Moments That Matter

Moments That Matter

Marking Transitions in Midlife and Beyond

RABBI LAURA GELLER
&
RABBI BETH LIEBERMAN

RABBI RICHARD F. ADDRESS, DMIN
Consulting Editor

Reform Judaism Publishing, a division of CCAR Press
Central Conference of American Rabbis
5786 NEW YORK 2025

Copyright © 2025 by the Central Conference of American Rabbis.
All rights reserved. No portion of this book may be copied in any form
for any purpose without the written permission of the Central Conference
of American Rabbis.

Published by Reform Judaism Publishing, a division of CCAR Press
Central Conference of American Rabbis
New York, NY
(212) 972-3636 | info@ccarpress.org | www.ccarpress.org

LIBRARY OF CONGRESS CATALOGING-IN-PUBLICATION DATA
Names: Geller, Laura, 1950– author. | Lieberman, Beth, 1962– author.
Title: Moments that matter: marking transitions in midlife and beyond / by
　Rabbi Laura Geller and Rabbi Beth Lieberman.
Description: First edition. | New York, NY: Published by Reform Judaism
　Publishing, a division of CCAR, Central Conference of American Rabbis
　Press, 2025. | Summary: "Moments That Matter offers a fresh perspective
　on life's later chapters, transforming them into opportunities for
　personal growth, meaning, and renewal. The chapters weave Jewish wisdom
　with practical rituals, interspersed with personal stories and ways to
　adapt each ceremony for a communal setting"—Provided by publisher.
Identifiers: LCCN 2025014849 (print) | LCCN 2025014850 (ebook) | ISBN
　9780881236644 (trade paperback) | ISBN 9780881236651 (ebook)
Subjects: LCSH: Aging–Religious aspects–Judaism. | Self-actualization
　(Psychology) in old age. | Self-realization in old age. | Older
　people—Conduct of life.
Classification: LCC BM540.A35 M66 2025 (print) | LCC BM540.A35 (ebook) |
　DDC 296/.084/6–dc23/eng/20250403
LC record available at https://lccn.loc.gov/2025014849
LC ebook record available at https://lccn.loc.gov/2025014850

Book interior designed and composed by Scott-Martin Kosofsky
　at The Philidor Company, Rhinebeck, NY. www.philidor.com
Cover design by Barbara Leff

Printed in the U.S.A.
10 9 8 7 6 5 4 3 2 1

To the memory of my beloved husband,
Richard A. Siegel, z"l,
and with love to our grandchildren,
Avery, Levi, Phoebe, Alice, and Nell,
and to their parents,
Joshua and Janelle Goldstein,
Elana Goldstein and Zach Rausnitz,
Ruth Siegel and Will Swanson.

—Laura

With love to my husband,
Chai,
and to our children,
Sarah and Hannah.
May your journeys be blessed and protected, always.
And to Kate Meyer, z"l,
who would have loved this book.

—Beth

Contents

Foreword   ix
   Casper ter Kuile

In Gratitude   xiii

Introduction   xvii

PART ONE: *Becoming an Elder*
1. Celebrating a Milestone Birthday   3
2. Committing to a Purposeful New Focus   11
3. From Retirement to Renewment   19
4. Embracing the Joy of Facing Finitude   29

PART TWO: *Loved Ones*
5. Launching Children   37
6. Relaunching Ourselves   43
7. Celebrating Friendship   49
8. Renewing Partnership Vows   57
9. Becoming a Grandparent/Grandfriend   65
10. Finalizing a Separation or Divorce   75
11. Moving Forward After the Death of a Partner   83
12. Beginning a New Relationship   91

PART THREE: *Bodies Changing, Caregiving, and Caregetting*
13. Needing Something to Lean On   99
14. Coming Out with Memory Loss   107
15. Becoming a Caregiver or a Caregetter   119
16. Starting or Ending Medical Treatment   129

PART FOUR: *Community*

17 Saying Goodbye to a Parent's Home ... 139
18 Decluttering or Downsizing Your Home ... 145
19 Leaving Your Home ... 149
20 Moving into a New Community and a New Home ... 157

A Concluding Thought ... 165

Notes ... 167

About the Authors ... 177

Foreword

Casper ter Kuile

Ritual makes the invisible, visible.

Through the intentional sequencing of sound, movement, taste, sight, and smell, our everyday lives are infused with meaning. From the simple singing of "Happy Birthday" to the multiday journey of the High Holy Days, ritual can transport us from the mundane to the magical. It adds contour and texture. Ritual brings us toward one another and helps us journey inward to our deepest mysteries. Ritual guides us back to the unknown longing of our hearts in a culture that pays little attention to stillness and rarely rewards reflection. And in this time of digital primacy—where more and more of us work, play, and connect online—it has become more valuable than ever to experience the power of physical presence, of making meaning ritually of our lives, in person.

Learning how to shape a ritual—how to hold space for others to experience it—is therefore a life skill of profound importance. With the advent of AI comes a profound cultural shift, and it is not farfetched to say that one purpose for religious traditions in the future will be to help us remember what it is that actually makes us human—what is at the very heart of who we are as living beings.

At least one part of that answer is ritual-making. Since the dawn of time, we humans have been ritual-makers. Indeed, anthropologists tell us, we created ritual before we used language itself. Ritual is able to express the movement of the soul—those yearnings we cannot say and may not even know. How often have you heard someone exclaim after singing together or sharing silence in meditation, "I didn't realize how much I needed that!" As Mary Douglas wrote so well, "There are some things we cannot experience without ritual."[1]

But ritual does more than give shape to our longings. It marks time. The Bloomsbury Group art critic Clive Bell put it like this: "Ritual gives significance to the stuff of our days—eating and drinking, sowing and harvesting, birth and death, our experience of time."[2] Ritual helps us remember the moments that matter—which is why I am so delighted to celebrate Rabbi Laura Geller and Rabbi Beth Lieberman's wise new book.

I was a graduate student at Harvard Divinity School when I first learned of Rabbi Geller, and I am delighted to say that just about every original thought I thought I might have is one she had already written about—or built a new project around! Her pioneering vision in congregational leadership at Temple Emanuel is matched only by her ritual imagination. Throughout her rabbinate, Rabbi Geller has insisted that the Torah of tradition must also be informed by the Torah of our lives; she understands that our lived experience is a rich source of religious insight. That same creative spirit simmers through the pages of this book. We live amid new technologies and new social realities—is it not self-evident that we will need new rituals too? And, for those questioning the validity of ritual creativity, was not every tradition once an innovation?

Each of the rituals featured here, including becoming a grandparent, acknowledging memory loss, or finalizing a divorce, marks a life transition. Rabbis Geller and Lieberman have accompanied so many people through these changes. They know the stories. And they know what's ritually missing in these meaningful moments. What blessing is there for marking a milestone birthday? For celebrating a friendship after fifty years? For honoring the ending of medical treatment? This book gives the soul-needs of those moments shape and structure. It helps make the invisible, visible.

But just as nearly half of American couples turn to a friend to officiate their wedding instead of a traditional member of the clergy, so too those who seek rituals in older life will likely look not only to religious leaders, but to friends and family members also. That's why I celebrate that this book is packed not only with thought-provoking, imaginative storytelling and insight, but also with the practical guidance we each need to create these ritual moments in our own lives and in the lives of our communities. It offers a profoundly democratic model for ritual leadership, suggesting the ritual materials and offering short scripts for blessings and words to share with gathered loved ones.

Perhaps this project contributes to the beginning of a ritual renaissance. Everywhere, people—young and old—are searching for meaning and community. Corporations are drawing on ritual language to sell makeup and develop their fitness brands. Activists are integrating ritual guidance into their tool kits, and even urban planners are thinking about how rituals can create community cohesion. We feel the absence of ritual in our lives, and Rabbis Geller and Lieberman point toward how it is possible to feel, once again, its presence.

Amid this turn toward meaning-making, may this book serve its readers, rooting itself in its rich understanding of tradition, while spreading its wings with contextual creativity. May it guide and inspire. May it offer grounding and comfort. And may each of us remember that life is for living—that every moment matters.

Casper ter Kuile is the author of The Power of Ritual *and the co-founder of Sacred Design Lab, Nearness, and the hit podcast* Harry Potter and the Sacred Text. *His work has been featured in* The New York Times, The Washington Post, VICE, *and on NPR, and he has spoken widely on community trends, ritual, and emerging spirituality. He holds master degrees in divinity and in public policy from Harvard University and served as a Ministry Innovation Fellow at Harvard Divinity School from 2016 to 2021. He lives with his husband, Sean Lair, in New York.*

In Gratitude

Special thanks for their financial support:
Temple Emanuel of Beverly Hills
Textish Books

We have been truly blessed with the wisdom and support of these individuals and communities during (and some, for years leading up to) the creation of this book:

All those who have invited us to your communities to speak and teach about the topics in *Moments That Matter* and about *Getting Good at Getting Older*

All those who have trusted us with your stories

Rabbi Hara Person, chief executive of the Central Conference of American Rabbis, and the team at the CCAR Press: Rafael Chaiken, Rabbi Annie Villarreal-Belford, Deborah Smilow, and Raquel Fairweather-Gallie; also Debra Hirsch Corman, Michelle Kwitkin, Barbara Leff, and, of course, Scott-Martin Kosofsky

Consulting editor Rabbi Richard Address, a pioneer in bringing Jewish values to the field of creative aging

All those whose wisdom helped create the landscape for paying attention to the experience of active older adults: Rabbi Zalman Schachter-Shalomi, *z"l*, Rabbi Rachel Cowan, *z"l*, Dr. Linda Thal, Rabbi Dayle Friedman, Susan Berrin, Casper ter Kuile, Angie Thurston, Marc Freedman, Paul Irving, the board and staff of CoGenerate, Helen Dennis, Stuart Himmelfarb, David Elcott, Rabbi Alicia Magal, Rabbi Sid Schwarz, and David Behrman

As well as:
Lisa Berman
Ezra Bookman
Chai Village LA

Don Cervantes, Ellen Cervantes, and Jerry Witkovsky, z"l
Institute for Jewish Spirituality and its teachers, especially Rabbi Marc Margolius and Melila Hellner-Eshed
Jewish Grandparents Network, especially Terry Kaye
Jewish Women's Archive
Barbara Kline
Laura's *Chavurah*
Laura's Girl Cousins Group
Laura's beloved friends Ron Andiman, Ross Brann, Eileen Yagoda, Isa Aron, Bill Aron, Frida Furman, Diane Katz, Cantor Sarah Sager, Scott Stone, Barbara Reisman, and Judith Resnik
Caryl Lieberman and Dr. Michael Theil
Dr. Lauren Muhlheim
Reverend Elizabeth Nordquist, Laura's spiritual director
Dr. Loraine K. Obler
One Table Together
Or Ami Village, The Middle at Or Ami
Recustom, especially Eileen Levinson and Rebecca Missel
Ritualwell
Rabbi Ruth Sohn and her Shabbat Meditation Group
Synagogue Village Network
The Torah Tribe of Temple Emanuel
Diane Vanette
The *Vatikot*—First-Generation Women Rabbis
Barri Waltcher
Hebrew Union College–Jewish Institute of Religion rabbinical students Chayva Lehrman, Michael Walden, and Sarah Livschitz, who shared Laura's home as we worked on this project
Women's *Chevra Shas*
Women's Rabbinic Network, especially Rabbi Mary Zamore and Rabbi Elaine Rose Glickman

Other colleagues who inspired us:
Rabbi Jonathan Aaron
Rabbi Nina Bieber Feinstein

Rabbi Richard Camras
Rabbi Cantor Hillary Chorny
Rabbi Lisa Edwards and Tracy Moore
Rabbi Dr. Tamara Eskenazi
Rabbi Edward Feinstein
Rabbi Paul Kipnes
Carol Koransky
Rabbi Marion Lev Cohen
And especially Dr. Riv-Ellen Prell

And each other—for the trust, commitment, and friendship that made it especially sweet to bring our shared vision to fruition.

Introduction

I will carry you through these changes.
—an interpretive translation of Isaiah 46:4

Laura is in her seventies. She is a widow with grown kids, who live far away, and grandchildren up and down the West Coast. Beth is in her early sixties; she and her husband just became empty nesters. We are at different points on our respective life's journeys, yet both of us are part of a huge population of people who are creating a new stage of life, living thirty more years than earlier generations did. Those thirty years are not tacked on to the end of our lives, but rather fall in between midlife, when we raised our families and built our careers, and frail old age. It is not that we will be frail old-agers for thirty years or continuing to raise families (though of course some of us might). Instead, we will be active older adults.

There is no consensus about what to call this stage. We know it is the stage beyond midlife, but it is even hard to agree on how to define midlife. Is it fifty, assuming some of us might live to a hundred? Is it when we are invited to join AARP? Is it sixty-five, the age when Social Security kicks in? Perhaps midlife is not a chronological age at all, but the beginning of a new stage.

Some in this new stage are healthy and active, while others wrestle with physical challenges or illness; some are parents of adult children and may be grandparents, while some don't have children or grandchildren or don't have the relationship with them they might wish they had. Some are solo agers, while others have partners. Some are caregivers to people close to them. Some are straight and some are LGBTQ+. Some have discretionary resources, and some worry about financial futures. Those of us in this new stage are a diverse group and pioneers—the first generation in history to have not only such a long lifespan, but for many of us, a long health span with many years of relatively good health.

So, what do we call this stage? The third chapter? The encore years? Middlescence? Senescence? Chrysalis? The "I'm on my next to last dog" stage? And just as important, what do we call ourselves? Seniors? Elders? Active older adults? Seasoned? Perennials? Whatever we label it, whatever we call ourselves, one question jumps out at us: Now that there are more active years added to our lives, how do we add more life to our years? The Book of Psalms offers guidance: "Let us know how to make our days count, and sum them up in a heart of wisdom" (Psalm 90:12). This verse is challenging us to pay attention. The Hebrew phrase for paying attention is *sim lev*, which literally translates to "place your heart."

When we pay attention to the endings and beginnings in this stage of life's journey, we notice that all endings are also beginnings. This is why paying attention and marking moments is so important in this stage. Jewish tradition encourages us to say a hundred blessings a day—in other words, to stop one hundred times each day and pay attention. Before we bite into the apple in our hands, we can pause and ask ourselves: Who planted the tree where this apple grew? Who picked it? Who carried it to the grocery store where we bought it? What were their working conditions? How much were their wages? Whom ought we to thank for the labor that makes our enjoyment of the apple possible? And how are we connected to the Source of life that makes apples grow? Jewish tradition gives us a language for this—a myriad of traditional blessings. These include blessings when we reunite with a friend we haven't seen for a while, when we see flowers blooming, and when we gather to celebrate holidays with family and friends. Other religious traditions offer similar ways of paying attention and cultivating gratitude. Blessings like this can be part of a frame to experience these moments as ones of connection and transformation.

A classic way religious traditions help us mark moments is through intentional acts that are often called ritual. But ritual is not only religious; it can also be secular. We wake up in the morning to our seven o'clock alarm, make a cup of coffee, then sit on our favorite chair to read through the day's news—this is a ritual. When we invite friends or family over for a special meal, we might set the table with our best dishes and prepare everyone's favorite foods; this is also a ritual. How we sustain ourselves—whether through study, prayer, cultural outings, yoga classes, and the like—could all be called "ritual." By intentionally marking moments through secular rituals like these, we often feel a greater sense of security in a world filled with uncertainty. For others, reciting a blessing that links us to community or following a spiritual or cultural practice of another religious tradition adds to the moment.

Why is this important? Dacher Keltner, who has taught the science of happiness to hundreds of thousands of people online and at UC Berkeley where he is a professor of psychology, recalls that over the years "I have been asked one key question: How might I find deeper happiness?" His answer is as follows: "Find more community. Deepen your connections with others. Be with others in meaningful ways. Find rituals to organize your life. It will boost your happiness, give you greater joy, even add ten years to your life expectancy, science suggests. . . . Rituals, in my view, are patterned, repeated ways in which we enact the moral emotions—of compassion, gratitude, awe, bliss, empathy, ecstasy—that have been shaped by our hominid evolution and built up into the fabric of our culture through cultural evolution."[1]

This book focuses on specific kinds of ritual—the ones that help us at moments of transition. In classic anthropological theory, life-cycle rituals are those rituals or ceremonies that mark the passage of an individual from one stage of life to another or from one social role to another. While one might argue that ritual and ceremony mark transitions in different ways, we are using the words as synonyms.

Most of us know about life-cycle rituals. Childhood in particular is full of rituals that mark transitions: For Jews, there are ceremonies that bring children into the covenant, and for Christians, there is baptism. There are ceremonies that mark our movement from childhood to adolescence: Bet mitzvah, confirmation, quinceañera, and sweet-sixteen parties are some examples. Later, there are graduations and commencements. There are weddings. And then? Perhaps those of us with children or grandchildren relive these life-cycle moments through them, but of course not all of us have children or grandchildren or are able to participate the way we wish we could.

And what comes next?

Funeral.

Ironically, many of us will live more years between our weddings (if we had one) and our funerals than between our births and our weddings. Yet, there are no formal rituals during this unfolding and perhaps very long stage of life. What are important moments now and going forward that will help us notice what really matters to us as we grow older? What are the transitions from one social role to another?

Here are three examples that highlight the need for new rituals during this stage of life.

Daniel and Sue's Story

This brother and sister called their rabbi on the way to clean out their parents' apartment just after they moved their widowed mother into a nursing home. They asked, "What is the right prayer you say when you begin to close up your childhood home?" This is not a traditional life-cycle moment, but a powerful one nonetheless. The answer to their question was not in the rabbi's clergy handbook... yet. With their rabbi, Daniel and Sue created the right prayer and said it before they began their work; this simple ritual transformed the experience from a chore to a sacred act. Paying attention to this moment of transition was part of acknowledging a shift in their roles with their mother and with each other.

Penelope's Story

Penelope, a Buddhist who had been raised Christian, felt that her seventy-fifth birthday was a good time to reflect on the wisdom she had learned through her life experience and communicate that she wanted to be a wise elder. Her ritual centered around the presentation by a close friend of a wide belt, woven from cloth Penelope had carried with her as she immersed in the ocean before the ceremony. The friend said, "This cloth symbolizes your passage into elderhood, your affinity with the ocean, and the symbolic connection with the universal ocean, which we never left and of which we are always a part. You will wear this belt at the time of your death ceremony and as a talisman that will go with you thereafter." Paying attention to this "big birthday" meant thinking through what it meant to her to become an elder in her community of friends.

Frank's Story

After forty years of being a doctor in a small family practice, Frank was getting tired of his relentless schedule. And though he loved his work with patients, he was frustrated by the hospital with which he was affiliated and their expectation that he shift to electronic records. That kind of technology was never easy for him, and he didn't want to have to start to learn. He began to cut back his hours to have more time for his hobbies of painting and collage, but the part-time practice wasn't making enough money to cover all the costs of running an office, like malpractice insurance and paying his staff. After six months of this part-time work, Frank stepped back and looked over the paintings he had created. At that moment he realized that this was what brought him joy. With his wife's support, he invited a small group of his closest friends and family to his home to see his paintings. He wanted his friends to understand that this was a major new direction in his life and to give him their blessings. This ritual allowed him to claim a new identity as an artist.

PAYING ATTENTION to these transitions underscores that everything changes. It keeps us from getting stuck in the denial to which many of us cling in order to avoid acknowledging that we are getting older. It helps us continue to move forward in our lives.

Each of the stories and rituals described above follows a similar pattern. First, they named the situation. For Daniel and Sue, it was "We're moving Mom to a nursing home." Penelope acknowledged, "I'm turning seventy-five." Frank realized, "I'm changing my priorities."

Second, they acknowledged the complicated feelings their situations evoked. Daniel and Sue said, "Moving Mom to a nursing home is a huge relief, but it is also sad. She was once so powerful in our lives, and now our roles have reversed and we are parenting her. At least we don't have to worry about her safety anymore. But for her, the loss of independence is painful." Penelope asserted, "At seventy-five, I feel ready to reflect on the wisdom I have acquired through my life experience. I want to claim the status of elder in the presence of family and friends who have been part of my community and thank them for helping to bring me to this moment. But I also know that there is so much less time ahead than there was behind and that I will die. How do I face the truth of my mortality and of impermanence?" Frank admitted, "I'm ready to retire from the concerns that have occupied my life and my attention for so many years. I remember the joy I had as a child when I was taking drawing and painting classes. I haven't had time to nurture those talents. I think I am ready to take the risk of focusing my energy on making art, but I'm also scared. What if I don't really have the talent to do it well? How will I measure my success? What if my friends think this is just indulgence?"

The third step after naming the situation and acknowledging the complicated feelings is to think about ritual as a way to resolve the complication. Resolution involves not denying the often-conflicting feelings, but rather opening to the fullness of the moment and holding multiple feelings at the same time—loss and joy, confusion and clarity, fear and confidence. Through the ceremony we create, we give ourselves the spaciousness to keep moving forward.

Rituals are not magic. While a ritual helps us mark a moment, it is not a spell that can wipe away something bad or predict the future. But rituals can help us pay attention, transform our experiences, and resolve complicated feelings.

Yes, we are creating new rituals. We are innovating what might become new traditions. We are celebrating the truth that all religious and secular traditions have evolved and changed over time in response to changing life circumstances. Think about the many new rituals in Judaism and other religious communities that have been influenced by the insights of feminism—covenant ceremonies for girls, blessing for menarche, and birth rituals like burying an umbilical cord. Even in the Talmud, more than fifteen hundred years ago, we learn that when there is a question as to what the law is, the Talmud advises, "Go out and see what the people are doing" (Babylonian Talmud, *B'rachot* 45a).

Who Is This Book For?

First and foremost, this book is written for active adults who want to mark an important moment of transition. You are the "subjects" of the ritual that you will create. We also hope that clergy who want to imagine how to create ways to mark these moments within their faith communities will find this book meaningful and useful.

This is a book for Jews who are affiliated with a faith community like a synagogue or with a cultural institution like a Jewish Community Center. It is also for those who prefer to express their connection to Judaism through the arts, culture, and food. It's also for those who are Jewish-adjacent—that is, someone connected to a Jewish family or community though they themselves are of another faith or background. It's for solo agers and those with partners, those with adult children and grandchildren and those without, those who are straight and those who are LGBTQ+. It's a book for people who consider themselves secular or "spiritual but not religious." It's a book for anyone who is curious about how to make these new steps in life's journey more meaningful—whether it is for themselves or someone they love, like a parent or a beloved friend.

This book is for anyone, Jewish or not, who has the curiosity and chutzpah to create new ritual patterns and pathways that can add meaning to their lives. It is for anyone who, in the words of author Angeles Arrien, consider themselves to be in the second half of life—the ultimate initiation—in which "we encounter new, unexpected, unfamiliar, and unknowable moments that remind us that we are a sacred mystery made manifest. If we truly understand what is required of us at this stage, we are blessed with an enormous opportunity to develop and embody wisdom and character. We enjoy limitless possibilities to restore, renew, and heal ourselves. And because of our increased longevity, for the first time in history we also have the opportunity to create a map of spiritual maturity for future generations to use as they enter their own later years."[2]

The Structure

Typical life-cycle books are organized around chronology, with one life-cycle ritual following another in the order the transition being marked occurs. But in the stages of midlife and beyond there is no chronology. Some people retire at sixty-five, others in their fifties, seventies, or eighties. For some a big birthday is sixty, or eighty, or the year after a parent might have died. A renewal of vows might happen after thirty years or after fifty years of an intimate partnership. Celebrating a friendship or beginning a new relationship could happen at any time. So instead of chronology, we chose themes that become more important as one grows older: elderhood, connections and community, changes in our bodies, and leaving, remaking, and finding home in new ways. The first, third, and fourth parts each contain four rituals, while relationships with loved ones contain seven. Given all we are learning about loneliness and isolation and how important cultivating and deepening connections with other people are—especially at this life stage—it is not a surprise to see more rituals for these moments than in the other three parts.

The parts are divided into chapters, each one focusing on a transition during a "moment that matters." It begins with a short word of wisdom from a sacred text or more contemporary writer. Next is a very short introduction into this particular moment, designed to make the purpose of the ritual clear. Following that are some questions for the subject of the ritual to consider as they adapt the ritual template for their own use.

The ritual template—which includes suggestions about the time, place, people, and material or objects to be used in the ritual—is next. The template often borrows a framing and blessings from a traditional Jewish ceremony such as *Havdalah*. *Havdalah* is the ceremony that marks the end of Shabbat with wine, spices, and candlelight, serving as a metaphor for moving from one stage—Shabbat—into a new one—the rest of the week, bringing the sweetness of what is being left behind into the new stage. We find this to be a powerful goal of rituals for this stage of life. We also borrow framing from the Passover seder, the ritual meal that tells the story of the Exodus from Egypt, reimagining it as a metaphor for coming out of a narrow place. Other examples of rituals that lend their framing or blessings include the prayer for a journey, placing of a mezuzah on a doorpost, or breaking a glass during a wedding. In each case we are using established Jewish ritual as a jumping-off point for a new ritual template that will frame this moment that matters.

After the template, there will be a few stories of different ways people have marked the particular moment in their lives. Some of the stories are first-person narratives from the people who experienced the event and are indicated by quotation marks; some are our descriptions of events others experienced. We are grateful to each person who shared their story with us.

It is important to us to show that the template is only one of many different ways to think about how to mark a moment. We hope the templates we offer here will spark your own creativity as you adjust, refine, or completely reimagine the rituals described in each section. We also hope that clergy might adapt these rituals for communal settings.

All endings are beginnings. Doors close and doors can open if we make our days count and our moments matter. As rabbis and active older adults ourselves, we know that this journey does not stop. Consider this book as the invitation to join us and all those who have shared their stories as we continue the journey, stage by stage, together.

Enjoy the journey.

PART ONE
Becoming an Elder

CHAPTER 1

Celebrating a Milestone Birthday

> Elderhood, properly understood, is actually
> a delicious form of liberation.[1]
> —Bill Thomas, MD

Introduction

WHILE JEWISH TRADITION originally didn't mark birthdays, we in North America do. Turning eighteen or twenty-one conveys a new legal status and brings new privileges. Fifty brings membership in the AARP. Sixty-five brings the blessing of Medicare. As people grow older and begin to accept that there is less time ahead than behind, all birthdays seem important, especially the decade ones. In fact, some research suggests that the year before the "big" birthday often initiates a time of reflection in preparation. One of the earliest adult milestone birthday ceremonies in contemporary Jewish tradition was created by feminist scholar Savina Teubal (with help from Debbie Friedman, Drorah Setel, and Marcia Falk) when Savina was about to turn sixty. The well-known song *L'chi Lach* (by Debbie Friedman and Drorah Setel) was composed for this occasion.

The ancient text *Pirkei Avot* teaches us, "A fifty-year-old can offer counsel; a sixty-year-old attains seniority [*ziknah*, wisdom that comes from life experience]; a seventy-year-old attains ripe old age [*seivah*, fullness of age]; an eighty-year-old shows strength [*g'vurah*]; a ninety-year-old becomes stooped over" (5:25). The ritual we offer in this chapter is designed for just that: to give counsel, to share the wisdom that comes from life experience, and to be present in the fullness of age.

Questions to Consider
- What does this birthday mean to you?
- If you were to reframe the question "How old are you?" to "What were some significant periods or experiences in your life that shaped who you are?" how might this change your perspective about this birthday?

The Gathering[2]

Time and Place

This ceremony can take place anywhere that participants can be seated around tables for a symbolic meal and a conversation. It can be held near a major birthday in your later years or a birthday that has special significance (such as the year you turn the same age as one of your parents when they died).

People

Gather friends and family.

Materials

Four cups or glasses for each participant
  (or one each that can be rinsed out between drinks)
Milk
Sangria
Champagne
Water

Ritual

Once everyone is seated around a table with four cups at their place setting, a participant reads:

לִמְנוֹת יָמֵינוּ כֵּן הוֹדַע, וְנָבִא לְבַב חָכְמָה.

Limnot yameinu kein hoda, v'navi l'vav chochmah.
Teach us to count our days rightly,
that we may obtain a wise heart. (Psalm 90:12)

The guest of honor reads the following:

I am growing older. Admitting that truth to myself and to you is complicated. In some ways I still feel that I am the twenty-year-old I once was (or the thirty-year-old, or the forty-year-old). And I also know that I am who I am now because of all the choices I have made along life's journey. This is a moment of looking back and of looking forward. Taking inspiration from a Passover seder or a Tu BiSh'vat seder, today we are celebrating a wisdom seder. On our table we have milk, sangria, champagne, and water, with four cups for each person. Please pour the milk into the first cup.

Our first cup—a cup of milk—represents childhood. Milk, known as a symbol for nourishment of babies and young children, represents innocence.

Go around the table(s) and invite participants to share a story or a recollection of their childhood that contributes to their sense of wisdom that is now theirs.

Recite this blessing for milk:

בָּרוּךְ אַתָּה, יְיָ, אֱלֹהֵינוּ מֶלֶךְ הָעוֹלָם, שֶׁהַכֹּל נִהְיֶה בִּדְבָרוֹ.

Baruch atah, Adonai, Eloheinu Melech haolam, shehakol nih'yeh bidvaro.

Source of life and all Creation—at Your word all came to be.

The guest of honor reads the following:

The second cup—a cup of sangria—symbolizes the tween, teen, and young adult years. Wine mixed with fruit serves as a symbol of the sweetness of discovery paired with the headiness of life during those years.

Invite participants to share a story or an image of their tween, teen, and young adult self that contributes to the wisdom they hold today.

Recite this blessing for sangria:

בָּרוּךְ אַתָּה, יְיָ, אֱלֹהֵינוּ מֶלֶךְ הָעוֹלָם, בּוֹרֵא פְּרִי הַגָּפֶן.

Baruch atah, Adonai, Eloheinu Melech haolam, borei p'ri hagafen.

Blessed are You, Source of life and all Creation—
You create the fruit of the vine.

The guest of honor reads the following:

The third cup—a glass of champagne—honors our years of building an adult life, which might include a family and one or more careers. Champagne serves as a celebratory symbol of achievement or reaching a milestone.

Invite participants to share a story or an image of their building family or career that has contributed to the wisdom they possess today.

Recite this blessing for champagne:

בָּרוּךְ אַתָּה, יְיָ, אֱלֹהֵינוּ מֶלֶךְ הָעוֹלָם, בּוֹרֵא פְּרִי הַגָּפֶן.

Baruch atah, Adonai, Eloheinu Melech haolam, borei p'ri hagafen.
Blessed are You, Source of life and all Creation—
You create the fruit of the vine.

The guest of honor reads the following:

Finally, we celebrate this new stage of elderhood, over our fourth glass—a glass of water. Water, known for its life-giving properties, represents ultimate clarity of vision.

Recite this blessing for water:

בָּרוּךְ אַתָּה, יְיָ, אֱלֹהֵינוּ מֶלֶךְ הָעוֹלָם, שֶׁהַכֹּל נִהְיֶה בִּדְבָרוֹ.

Baruch atah, Adonai, Eloheinu Melech haolam, shehakol nih'yeh bidvaro.
Blessed are You, Source of life and all Creation—
at Your word all came to be.

Invite participants to share a story or an image of someone who is a role model of elderhood or what it means to them to claim the status of elder.

In conclusion, a participant reads:

The traditional Jewish birthday blessing is *Ad mei-ah v'esrim*, "May you live to be 120," just as Moses did. Let's join together with a contemporary reformulation that plays with the Biblical verse referring to Sarah's age. Genesis states that Sarah lived to be one hundred years and twenty years and seven years instead of saying that Sarah lived 127 years (Genesis 23:1). Why? The Rabbis suggest that at one hundred she was as youthful as she had been at twenty, and at twenty she was as energetic as she had been at seven.

Together we say:

Ad mei-ah k'esrim—may you live to be one hundred as though you were twenty—still active, engaged, curious, and grateful.

To close, everyone recites the *Shehecheyanu* blessing, which is typically said at milestone moments.

בָּרוּךְ אַתָּה, יְיָ, אֱלֹהֵינוּ מֶלֶךְ הָעוֹלָם,
שֶׁהֶחֱיָנוּ וְקִיְּמָנוּ וְהִגִּיעָנוּ לַזְּמַן הַזֶּה.

*Baruch atah, Adonai, Eloheinu Melech haolam,
shehecheyanu v'kiy'manu v'higianu laz'man hazeh.*

Blessed are You, Source of life and all Creation—You have kept us in life, sustained us, and brought us to this moment of a new beginning.

Shana's Story

Shana studied the story of God calling Avram and Sarai, telling them that they should leave the comfort of where they were and go to a place that God will show them (Genesis 12). Shana realized they were adults—mature adults, beginning the next stage of their journey. Like those ancestors, Shana shared with the few friends present what she wanted to let go of and what new promises she was making at the threshold of this next stage of life's journey.

Ron's Story

Though Ron has lived in Los Angeles for the past fifty years, he never lost his Brooklyn accent, and he never really left the landscape that shaped his experience. So, when his eightieth birthday approached, he knew he wanted to bring all of his children and grandchildren to Brooklyn for a roots trip. The trip was a year in the planning. As a tribute to how much his family loves him, they managed to find a week where all of them—adult children and their partners, grandchildren ranging in age from six to twenty-one—could accompany him on the pilgrimage. He took them all to the places he remembered most, including the building in which his family lived, the place where he and his friends played stoop ball, and the Polish Catholic church across the street. In front of each of these landmarks he told his stories. He even took them bird-watching on Jamaica Bay. Some birds fly far away but still return to the place they were born—the place that will always be home. Going "home" and sharing that home with those who matter so much in your life now is a powerful way to celebrate a big birthday.

Pauline's Story

"At seventy, I rappelled off the roof of the Ontario Airport Hotel building with harness, helmet, ropes, and the encouragement of family and friends. At seventy-five my husband and I bought a two-seater all-terrain vehicle and took off to be away from crowds, and headed to the Arizona desert to explore dirt roads, old mines, and whatever else interested us off the beaten path. My eightieth is coming up and I am thinking of my options—perhaps a hot air balloon over the wineries of Northern California or tandem airplane jump. Whatever I do will be an adventure, something to remember, and something about which my family and friends will say, 'Oh my, what's she up to now . . . but go, Granny! Go!'"

Marci's Story

"In honor of my fifty-eighth birthday, I asked people to invite me on walks of at least 5.8 miles. My plan was to do at least fifty-eight of them over the course of the year. That was the initial design. Then the walks started and I started to learn so much from the ritual. . . . The walks allow people to give me the gift of sharing places that are special to them—friends have taken me on walking tours of their towns or neighborhoods or favorite hikes, and food is always a part of it—I encourage snacking and meals along the way. The distance allows for deeper conversation than is possible over a coffee, meal, or phone call. They have also been excuses to learn about places I've been before but haven't explored with intention. With my friend Renee I walked all over Montclair, New Jersey, where she'd been living for twenty years. Before this I'd seen her house and perhaps a restaurant downtown; now I've seen her church and the soup kitchen where she volunteers, the local museum, and the schools her kids went to. With Sarah and Tony, I went on a dramatic walk in New York's Hudson Valley, a short drive from their home. With Katherine, we toured one section of Harlem, visiting four parks and countless historic mansions and rowhouses. Susan and I turned it into an excuse for a weekend away at a yoga retreat. Over time, I've realized I needed to adapt the project because some people I care about won't be able to walk 5.8 miles. So I now ask people to take me on any kind of excursion as long as we spend at least five hours and eight minutes together and have time for deep conversation. Because I post the '5.8s' on Instagram and Facebook, I've also heard from many people who want to join in without necessarily planning one. So I'll be hosting some '5.8s' where I plan the itinerary and will invite others to join. I'm sure there will be other tweaks by the time the calendar strikes fifty-nine. And then it'll be time for another ritual!"

For Clergy: Adapting for Communal Settings

Psalm 90:10 tells us that a person's life is seventy years. So, if you make it to eighty-three, it is as though you are thirteen again. With that insight, you may wish to create a new bet mitzvah tradition for your eighty-three-year-old congregants.

Rabbi Ed Feinstein, of the synagogue Valley Beth Shalom in Los Angeles, suggests holding a bet mitzvah ceremony on the occasion of every new decade after the first ceremony at the age of thirteen, even if someone did not have a bet mitzvah at thirteen.

At each birthday that celebrates a decade of their life (twenty, thirty, forty, and so on), the person celebrating would share their vision of meaning for this stage of their life, as a kind of living and evolving ethical will.

People celebrating their birthdays may wish to lead part of the Shabbat or weekday service, be honored with an *aliyah*, or give a brief talk about the Torah or haftarah portion. Then, people important to them can offer blessings. A perhaps unintended effect of this suggestion is that family and friends would come to shul to honor them.

Alternatively, at High Holiday services invite whoever will be celebrating what to them is a major birthday in the coming year to join a Wise Aging group. Have them center the group around the book *Wise Aging* by Rabbi Rachel Cowan and Dr. Linda Thal (Behrman House, 2015) or *Getting Good at Getting Older* by Richard Siegel and Rabbi Laura Geller (Behrman House, 2019). During the month of Elul, celebrate by creating a Torah scroll or a symbolic page of Talmud with words from each of the honorees and with blessings written from family and friends. One advantage of this is that the group will most likely be multi-generational.

Words of Wisdom
In the fullness of age may you still produce fruit;
may you continue to be full of sap and freshness.
—Psalm 92:15

CHAPTER 2

Committing to a Purposeful New Focus

> Don't ask yourself what the world needs. Ask what makes you come alive, and then go and do that. Because what the world needs is people who come alive.[1]
> —*Reverend Howard Thurman*

Introduction

THE JOURNEY of the Jewish people begins when our ancestors Avraham and Sarah are already seasoned older adults. The Biblical story describes that God called to them and said, "Go . . . to the land that I will show you . . . and it shall be a blessing" (Genesis 12:1–2). Whatever your theology or background, this story is a metaphor for choices we can make as we get older if we are open to the invitation or to the "call" of this moment. Many of us have spent much of the past decades building a career or perhaps raising a family. We have come to the stage in our lives that Erik Erikson, in *The Life Cycle Completed*, called "generativity," when the dominant motivation of our lives begins to shift from accumulating for ourselves—money, things, career success—to giving back and reinvigorating our natural inclination to do good for others.[2] At this stage, some of us want to make a firmer commitment than ever before to showing up for others—building bridges of care, engaging in civic activism, or otherwise strengthening our communities. Some of us want to reach across generations through mentoring or teaching younger folks or being a friendly presence for older folks. Others of us embark on a more internal journey, focusing on ongoing learning, a deepening spiritual practice, or sharing a creative passion.

You have prepared for this moment in many ways. You have listened to your desire to find a meaningful way to express what you want now. Perhaps you have researched groups or organizations to which you can make a meaningful contribution. You've spoken with friends, asked them what fills their days with purpose and what nourishes their soul. Maybe you have even found a few friends to join you in your new journey. Now you are ready to make a public commitment in the presence of loved ones, asking them to support you in this decision and even holding you accountable to your commitment.

Questions to Consider
- What commitment am I ready to make publicly?
- Why is this important to me?
- What support do I need in order to fulfill this commitment?

The Gathering

Time and Place

When you are ready to make a formal commitment to a new endeavor, in a location that symbolizes what you have been doing or what you intend to do—a community center, library, school, performance space, or museum—or your home.

People

Gather family and friends. You may also want to invite people who are already involved in a project you are interested in joining or those with whom you want to strengthen community, study, create, or engage in spiritual practice.

Materials

Objects or readings related to your new focus, brought by you and by participants

A shofar, gong, or hand drum

Ritual

The facilitator opens the gathering with the recording of a song the guest of honor loves that might resonate with the people in attendance. Afterward, a friend says:

> The Japanese word *Ikigai* means the purpose for which you wake up in the morning. Over the years there were different purposes—getting an education, succeeding at work, caring for family. Now, you are discerning a renewed purpose or possibly a new focus for

this next stage. Please tell us about it and why it is important to you.

The guest of honor shares their intention and purpose and an object that expresses their new focus.

Invite participants to share the object or a reading that they brought to the gathering. Each offering concludes with a personal blessing. For example, participants might say, "May you be blessed with _____ as your new focus unfolds."

The guest of honor offers a prayer:[3]

בָּרוּךְ שֶׁתִּתְחַדֵּשׁ עָלַי אֶת הָעֵסֶק הַזֶּה לְטוֹבָה וְלִבְרָכָה.

Baruch shet'chadeish alai et ha-eisek hazeh l'tovah v'livrachah.

May the new work I do be a source of goodness and blessing.

Follow with the *Shehecheyanu*:

בָּרוּךְ אַתָּה, יְיָ, אֱלֹהֵינוּ מֶלֶךְ הָעוֹלָם,
שֶׁהֶחֱיָנוּ וְקִיְּמָנוּ וְהִגִּיעָנוּ לַזְּמַן הַזֶּה.

*Baruch atah, Adonai, Eloheinu Melech haolam,
shehecheyanu v'kiy'manu v'higianu laz'man hazeh.*

Blessed are You, Source of life and all Creation—You have kept us in life, sustained us, and brought us to this moment of a new beginning.

Conclude together as everyone recites or sings *T'filat HaDerech*, also known as the Traveler's Prayer, by Debbie Friedman:

May you be blessed as you go on your way
May you be guided in peace
May you be blessed with health and joy
May this be your blessing, amen.
May you be sheltered by wings of peace
May you be kept in safety and in love
May grace and compassion find their way to every heart
May this be your blessing, amen.
Amen, may this be your blessing, amen.[4]

End with the sounding of the shofar (or other instrument).

Barbara's Story

"When I decided it was time to retire as a pediatrician, I wanted to be intentional about how I used my newly unstructured time. Yes, there was a regular yoga practice, adult-onset piano lessons, book and poetry groups, my collage art, more time with friends, and the delightful world of (long-distance) grandparenting. I had been active in many movements (Vietnam, civil rights, feminism) as a person who came of age in the sixties—and over the years my focus shifted to medical training, work, family, and the day-to-day-ness of life. At this juncture, I wanted to do something that would holistically channel my passion, my professional experience, and my politics while also fulfilling my own personal commitment to *tikkun olam* [repair of the world].

"When *Roe v. Wade* was overturned, I knew I wanted to find some path to action—to protect the right to an abortion for any pregnant person who chose to have one whatever the reason.... I went in search of the best way to participate in the organized post-Dobbs pro-choice pushback. I brainstormed with retired friends in medicine (abortions were not in my scope of care as a pediatrician); I participated in a 'lay' workshop learning about medical abortions and how to support women before, during, and after them; I participated in phone banks to encourage pro-choice voting on various state initiatives; I watched webinars about independent abortion clinics and providers around the country. I was educating myself while looking for my place, dipping my toe in many waters.

"Eventually, I recognized someone from my shul on one of the phone banks. She was involved in the *Tikkun Olam* subcommittee focused on saving democracy. After a brief discussion of like interests, we—along with two other women in the shul—formed the Abortion Access Action Group (AAAG).... Just over one year into this work, we've enlisted over sixty congregants, who have shown up in a variety of ways—large and small—to protect reproductive freedom."

Peter and Lesli's Story

When their daughter started kindergarten, Lesli got involved in the school's Parent-Faculty Club. "I was working part-time and had a schedule that allowed me to go to PFC board meetings, which I did. The other board members quickly found out that I had a finance background, so they asked me to serve as treasurer. It kind of snowballed after that until the president announced she was leaving, and I was asked to step into that role. I always thought, 'Well, I'm helping my kids get a great education,' and what happens is that you end up helping all the kids get a great education." Over time, Lesli volunteered for two district oversight committees, and as the kids entered high school, she served as the high school PFC president. After the kids went off to college, she served as synagogue president. "I really wanted to take some time off, but it's very hard to say no to your rabbi."

Peter started helping out behind the scenes, then got involved with the Boy Scouts. "Our son had joined and I wanted to see what was going on and be a part of that. It's one of those things where you start for your kids, and eventually you enjoy the community that you're working with, and you start offering that service to the others, and it just feels good as you start getting more and more involved." Eventually, Peter segued into local municipal work when a friend who was on the Calabasas Planning Commission started asking his thoughts on some projects, because he had some experience in the building industry. After enough conversations, she mentioned that a general plan advisory committee in the City of Calabasas was starting up.

Now that they are empty nesters, another door has opened. As Peter says, "I learned that when you start working in the volunteer world, and you actually do something, they come back and ask you again." Lesli is running for school board, and Peter, after having served on the city council, is now the city's mayor *pro tem*.

For Clergy: Adapting for Communal Settings

Clergy can invite an individual or a group of individuals sharing this transition to receive a special blessing, such as this adapted blessing from the life-cycle guide of the Central Conference of American Rabbis (CCAR):[5]

> May it be Your will, Source of life and all Creation, that You guide [name of person] safely on their journey and bestow blessing on the work of their hands. Grant grace, loving-kindness, and compassion to them and in the eyes of all whom they encounter on the way. Blessed are You, who watches over us on our journeys.

Individual or group of individuals respond:
> As I begin anew, let me rediscover the relationship between what I do and my deep purpose. Source of blessing, may my new work be a blessing, allowing me to discover and affirm the sacred in every day and realize my full potential.

Clergy can also share a teaching, which might include:

> רַבִּי יִרְמְיָה אָמַר הָעוֹסֵק בְּצָרְכֵי צִבּוּר כְּעוֹסֵק בְּדִבְרֵי תוֹרָה.
>
> Rabbi Yirm'yah says being occupied with community needs is equivalent to being occupied with matters of Torah (Jerusalem Talmud, *B'rachot* 5:1). Thus:
>
> בָּרוּךְ אַתָּה, יְיָ, אֱלֹהֵינוּ מֶלֶךְ הָעוֹלָם,
> אֲשֶׁר קִדְּשָׁנוּ בְּמִצְוֹתָיו, וְצִוָּנוּ לַעֲסוֹק בְּצָרְכֵי צִבּוּר.
>
> *Baruch atah, Adonai, Eloheinu Melech haolam,*
> *asher kid'shanu b'mitzvotav, v'tzivanu laasok b'tzorchei tzibur.*
>
> Blessed are You, Source of life and all Creation—
> You command us to engage in the needs of the community.

Words of Wisdom

The opposite of old is not young. The opposite of old is new. As long as we can experience the new, we will gloriously inhabit all of the ages that we are and welcome all of the dreams that we have.[6]

—*SARK*

CHAPTER 3

From Retirement to Renewment

> To take the first step—
> To sing a new song—
> Is to close one's eyes
> and dive
> into unknown waters.
> For a moment knowing nothing risking all—
> But then to discover
>
> The waters are friendly
> The ground is firm.
> And the song—
> the song rises again.[1]
> —*Rabbi Ruth Sohn*

Introduction

WHAT A VAST ARRAY of experiences and opportunities—the good as well as the not-so-good—make up a professional life! For some of us, forty or fifty years of paid work have shaped our days and our lives. How do we leave that work in a way that feels right and that honors our larger vision of what matters most?

Marking this moment is like a career review. It allows us to take stock of the important moments of building our professional lives, as well as to reflect on lessons learned from those we met along the way and what our impact has been on others. To do this in front of beloved witnesses will allow them to support us and to accompany us on the road that lies ahead.

Questions to Consider

Reflect on and write down your answers to these questions in preparation for this ritual:

- What were your professional roles and responsibilities?

- ❧ Whom did you influence, and who influenced you?
- ❧ What were the main things you learned over the span of your working life?

Time and Place

Choose a time after you have made the decision to retire. This ritual can take place in your home, the home of a friend, or some other place that might be meaningful to you.

People

Gather friends and family.

Materials

Havdalah candle or three strands of wax with wicks that can be woven together.

Your answers to the "questions to consider" above.

Ritual[2]

As people gather, play music that captures your feelings about this transition.

A facilitator or participant reads this poem:

For Retirement
This is where your life has arrived,
After all the years of effort and toil;
Look back with graciousness and thanks
On all your great and quiet achievements.
You stand on the shore of new invitation
To open your life to what is left undone;
Let your heart enjoy a different rhythm
When drawn to the wonder of other horizons.
Have the courage for a new approach to time;
Allow it to slow until you find freedom
To draw alongside the mystery you hold
And befriend your own beauty of soul.
Now is the time to enjoy your heart's desire,
To live the dreams you've waited for,

To awaken the depths beyond your work
And enter into your infinite source.³
— *John O'Donohue*

The facilitator sets the context through the metaphor of *Havdalah* and says:

> *Havdalah* acknowledges the transitional moment of the weekly cycle, when we leave the safety and sanctity of Shabbat to return to the world and face its joys, difficulties, and challenges. Like *Havdalah*, retirement is also a transition. The guest of honor finds themself in between full-time work and whatever might come next.

For the first thirty or so years of our lives, our focus is on creating identity, figuring out who we are, who we are going to be with, and how we are going to move forward. The next thirty or so years center around productivity, fulfilling the vision of who we—in our youth—thought we would be in our adulthood, and establishing ourselves through work and family life. The next span of years is where we are now—retirement, which is about reframing who we are. It is the time to discern how we can contribute to the world in a way that allows us take all of the gifts that we have both inherited and formed in our own work and apply them in a way that can better ourself, our family, our community, and the world.

The guest of honor shares some thoughts about three aspects of their professional life:
1. Where did you work; what roles did you play?
2. Which people influenced you; who have you influenced and in what ways?
3. What lessons have you learned over time?

Invite guests to share good wishes and, if so moved, words of wisdom for the guest of honor.

The guest of honor then weaves the *Havdalah* candle (or holds one up), noting how the three wicks being braided together symbolize integrating their past and their present in order to be able to create all of the tomorrows they will be blessed to shape. So, in this liminal moment, the guest of honor gathers up their past, takes it into their present, and uses it to create a vision for their hopes going forward in the future.

The guest of honor lights the candle and all present say this adapted *Havdalah* blessing:

בָּרוּךְ אַתָּה, יְיָ, אֱלֹהֵינוּ מֶלֶךְ הָעוֹלָם,
הַמַּבְדִּיל בֵּין עָמָל לְחַיֵּי מְנוּחָה.

*Baruch atah, Adonai, Eloheinu Melech haolam,
hamavdil bein amal l'chayei m'nuchah.*

Blessed are You, Source of life and all Creation—You separate the world of work from the new freedom to choose our endeavors, giving us the opportunity to carve out the kind of retirement only we can design.

Together, say: Amen!

The guest of honor then blows out the candle.

Moshe's Story

Your hand is slipping from my fingers.
I have held it for decades,
Through stinging sandstorms and torrential floods,
And times of humidity that stifled breath,
And some seasons of puff cotton clouds.
"How long have you been my patient?" I ask.
"Let me put it this way," she says.
"When I first met you I was thirty years old.
And now I am seventy."
"You are a part of my life," I tell her.
In my mind I am confirming that this is not what is called a
 "transactional relationship."
"We are bound up together," I tell her.
"We are family," she says.
"Yes," I say. "Family."

For some it is hand holding.
For some it is ear whispering.
For some it is gently pushing through a narrow doorway.
For some it is touching and speaking to a blank wall.
For some it is a dance.
For some it is a conversation in competing arias.
For some it is like reading a book and writing a book report.
For some it is like becoming enchanted by the plaintive call of a bird that I cannot locate in the foliage.

I look at my schedule in the last month.
I read the name of each patient I saw.
And as I read each name, I call up their image.
And their demeanor and their mannerisms, their way of speech.
Matthew E, Xena F, Susan U, Mary E, Bertil N
Their cognitive idiosyncrasies, their gait disturbances.
I know the vibration sensitivity of their toes, their visual field deficits.
Lorena G, Abe B, Marc F, Jack W, Ted L, Alvin R
Facial asymmetries, reflex losses,
This one's tremor, that one's dyskinesias, that one's chorea.
Carrie B, Susan C, Danny S, Helaine P, Chaya K
I know their spouses, their significant others, their aides,
Their wheelchairs, their single point canes, wide base canes, hiking staffs,
Front-wheeled walkers, four-wheeling walkers, reverse braking walkers.
Sang C, Janet A, Jerome M, Stuart K, Sheri K, Martha W
I have walked with them, months, years, decades.
Their lives have unspooled before my eyes.
Caroline S, Jo H, Don C, Susan O, Judy W, Elinoor A

I want to stay with them.
I want to know what happens next.

I am on the Plains of Moab at a cliff edge overlooking the
  Jordan Valley.
Not for no reason was I named Moshe.
My journey with my patients is halted here. My FOMO
  is frustrated.
But unlike my namesake of yore
With trepidation I will pick up my staff and turn back into the
  wilderness.
I will discover what delights await me
In my own Promised Land.[4]

—Ronald M. Andiman

Loraine's Story

"I thought to focus my ritual marking the transition to retirement around my address block: the set of lines one can have turn up at the end of every letter or email that include one's full name, title, address, phone number, and so on. I realized giving that up would feel like a big loss for me. Actually, it turns out I don't even have to give it up; I just turned the 'Distinguished Professor' title into 'Distinguished Professor Emerita.' With this change, I signal the identity shift from the great importance of my work from which I will be moving to the other aspects of my identity I will develop further in the next stage of my life.

"As I did this, I expressed deep gratitude to many individuals: to the many professors who stimulated my thinking and encouraged me, to my many colleague-friends in our field and outside it, to my parents who modeled aspects of an intellectual life, and to so many religious leaders—those rabbis, cantors, and teachers who have inspired me, giving me the gift of prayer as song and interpretation as something we all can do. I especially shared gratitude to my life partner, who challenged and challenges me in so many productive ways, as our son does too.

"With this modification of my title, then, I acknowledged with great appreciation all I had been given to prepare me for my work life during these wonderful adult years to date and all that I had been able to accomplish. I acknowledged the importance of my academic sabbaticals, which permitted less-pressured time to think about and try out retirement activities. In addition, discussions with fellow members of Lab/Shul's GENerate cohort and a biweekly gathering of older feminists has helped me prepare for the Big Final Exam beyond retirement. That exam will be living purposely as an elder and approaching dying and death in ways I'd feel good about, to the extent I have any say in the matter!"

Danny's Story

Rabbi Daniel Roberts is not one for many regrets—except one that stands out. After deciding to retire from being a congregational rabbi, he stumbled happily into retirement. He wishes that he had done a ritual to mark the end of his career.

Danny experienced loneliness after he left the pulpit. Not only did he miss the nearly constant personal interactions that had shaped his working days, but the path to his goodbye felt solitary too. He wished he could have had a cohort or a *chavurah* of people who were going through something similar. In addition, he realized that he should have done something to concretize the moment of transition—so he wrote a ritual for retirement.

How will you identify yourself now? A member of Shomrei Torah Synagogue in Los Angeles changed his LinkedIn profile from his corporate title to founder and CEO of a new company called Geezer Guitar Pickers.

The ritual is meant to be done in fellowship, ideally with one's family and friends. It is important for the honoree to talk about themself, to reflect on their accomplishments with pride, and to draw a road map to the next stop on their journey, but the real magic to this ritual is having your people be present with you. Retirement, like marriage, is a time to transition with the full witness of community. The ritual begins with a few sacred objects: challah, wine, and a candle. The script asks the retiree to acknowledge the holiness of the occasion and commences with the blessing of *Shehecheyanu,* thanking God for allowing them to reach this moment. The retiree then recalls with gratitude their parents, their partner, and any children who might have accompanied them to this stage. Danny references the sacred text from *B'reishit* in which God calls upon Abraham and Sarah to take a journey into the unknown, with the promise of added blessings. The honoree then declares, "I did go forth to make my way in life . . . to a world in which I could be a blessing to my spouse, friends, and people who were significant. Indeed, God's promise of being a blessing was fulfilled! I feel I touched the lives of so many [naming some] by completing my life's task up until this moment." There is a pivot, then, to anticipation of the days to come, accompanied by the ritual action of lighting a candle and a prayer that one may be a light of "justice and morality. . . strength and guidance, a light of leadership and support." The ritual closes with an adaptation of the Traveler's Prayer and perhaps a few additional readings if anyone at the gathering is so moved.

For Clergy: Adapting for Communal Settings

Honor all members who have retired recently on a Shabbat with a communal *aliyah* (ascending to offer the Torah blessings). Guide them in saying this blessing:[5]

> *Hineini.* Here I stand, on the way to the next step in my journey, knowing I can continue creating a full life for myself, knowing that I have a circle of loved and loving ones who will celebrate my endeavors, knowing that I am sheltered beneath the wings of the *Shechinah,* knowing my own power.

בָּרוּךְ אַתָּה, יְיָ, אֱלֹהֵינוּ מֶלֶךְ הָעוֹלָם,
שֶׁהֶחֱיָנוּ וְקִיְּמָנוּ וְהִגִּיעָנוּ לַזְּמַן הַזֶּה.

Baruch atah, Adonai, Eloheinu Melech haolam,
shehecheyanu v'kiy'manu v'higianu laz'man hazeh.

Blessed are You, Source of life and all Creation—You have kept us in life, sustained us, and brought us to this moment of a new beginning.

Words of Wisdom
Tell me, what is it you plan to do
with your one wild and precious life?[6]
—*Mary Oliver*

CHAPTER 4
Embracing the Joy of Facing Finitude

> I've come to understand that though the impermanence of life can be scary and sad, it also gives value to each moment. The present is what matters. I can't bring back the past and the future is basically out of my control. And the present is full of so much that is good. I am really happy.[1]
> —Rabbi Rachel Cowan

Introduction

THE BAD NEWS is that the death rate appears to be holding steady at 100 percent. You have come to the moment in your life when you stop saying "If I die . . ." and begin to say and actually believe that the correct formulation is "When I die. . . ." Different religious traditions have different ways of dealing with finitude. Judaism's holiest day, Yom Kippur, is a symbolic confrontation with death. Many Jews dress in a white shroud in which they will someday be buried and refrain from eating, drinking, bathing, being intimate with their partners, or wearing leather shoes, because, according to one explanation, corpses don't need shoes. A central liturgical text of Yom Kippur is the *Un'taneh Tokef*, a problematic medieval poem that asks, "Who will live and who will die; who will reach the ripeness of age, who will be taken before their time; who by fire and who by water; who by war and who by beast; who by famine and who by drought; who by earthquake and who by plague?"[2] Leonard Cohen adds, "Who by very slow decay?"[3] The answer is: You. You will die. Maybe this year. Maybe in thirty years, but still, you will die. We don't know when or what will cause it. But at this stage of our lives, we realize that there is less time ahead than there was behind. A challenge of facing finitude is to not only think about what you would still like to accomplish—your bucket list—but also, and just as important, what you have accomplished in your life so far and how you want to share that legacy. An important tool to explore is the tradition of writing an ethical will or forever letter.

Questions to Consider
- If you were to write your own obituary or design your own tombstone, what would you want it to say?
- If you were to die tonight, what would you regret?
- As you reflect on your life so far, what has brought you joy in your life? As you look forward into the future, what do you imagine will bring you joy?
- With whom do you want to share these thoughts?
- Are you willing to write an ethical will or forever letter?

What Is an Ethical Will?

Most of us write a last will and testament to be assured of a home for our possessions. An increasing number of us write a living will to outline our wishes for end-of-life medical care. Yet how many of us write an ethical will—a letter to those we leave behind, passing on our ethical values and ideals?

The ethical will was a popular form of literature in medieval Jewish communities (although it has existed as a form since ancient times). Parents wrote these letters to their children in order to prescribe a set of behaviors and religious practices that would guide their children to live meaningful lives. And so, today's ethical wills are a part of a long chain of Jewish tradition.

Rabbi Elana Zaiman, in her book *The Forever Letter*, teaches a modern way to do this, which enables us to "to communicate what we believe to those we love . . . to share our personal experiences, histories, and stories, to highlight our values, to forgive and to ask for forgiveness, to state hard truths, to state our ultimate truth, [and] to offer blessings."[4]

What is important to keep in mind, according to Zaiman, is that "when we share our personal experiences in a forever letter, we invite the people we love into our lives so they can better understand us and perhaps come to better understand themselves. We do this not to convince them to make the same choices in their lives that we made in ours, though we might hope they do. . . . We do this to explain ourselves, to connect, and to make an offering of love that we hope will help our words to be heard from a place of love."⁵

The Gathering
Time and Place

Choose a quiet place—your home or the home of a family member, after you have written an ethical will.

People

Invite those closest to you.

Materials

The ethical will/forever letter you have written

Ritual

Invite close family/friends to sit in a circle.

Share with those present why you chose to write an ethical will/forever letter.

Read it aloud.

Those present respond with one-word blessings for you.

Share a good meal.

Gabe's Story

"Now in my mid-seventies, as I look back over my life there is one thing I do regret: selling my Nvidia stock in 2008. . . . Had I held on to even a little I would be very rich now. To me, 'facing finitude' means that I acknowledge having made some unwise decisions but, at the same time, I know I also made good decisions. My spiritual and emotional work now as I look ahead is to reframe my focus from what I got wrong or failed to accomplish to focusing on gratitude for all I have accomplished and all that makes me feel good about life. My life has not been perfect, but it has been pretty good. My new mantra is the teaching from *Pirkei*

Avot: 'Who is rich? One who is content with what one has' (4:1). Facing finitude graciously is learning to be content with who I am now and being able to look forward to an unknown future with curiosity. I haven't done a ritual around this . . . but even admitting it through this story feels something akin to a way to mark what it teaches me."

Ed's Story

"There are 5,485 verses in a Torah scroll—tens of thousands of words, more than a hundred thousand handwritten letters. According to tradition, if any one letter, in any word, in any verse, is defaced or erased, the entire Torah is *pasul*, invalid, and may not be read. A Torah missing even the tiniest *yod* is set aside. Why such an obsession? A Chasidic tradition teaches that each letter stands for one human soul. Each individual human being carries one letter of God's message into the world. Just as the loss of the tiniest letter invalidates an entire Torah scroll, losing one human being renders God's message indecipherable. You carry part of God's message. But do you know what it is? Have you discovered it? Have you decoded your part of the message? Have you delivered it?

"As a rabbi, I frequently accompany families as they grieve. I ask them to share the stories and wisdom of their loved ones' lives. And I am frequently surprised how little they know. They can recount with precision the history of declining health, but they have no notion of the soul—the inner life, the moral struggles, the deepest values of the one whom they love. They know little of the poetry of the soul. 'My dad was unremarkable,' a son explains. 'He worked all the time, cared for Mom, built us this home, but nothing heroic, Rabbi. I'm afraid there's little to say about him.' Really? Nothing heroic in his devotion, commitment, care? Your loved ones deserve to know your inner truth. Leave it for them so they might cherish it."

For Clergy: Adapting for Communal Settings
Clergy might offer a class in writing ethical wills. When the class has concluded, invite those who participated to share publicly some of what they wrote, if they are comfortable, or simply to receive a blessing from the clergy.

Words of Wisdom
I leave you not everything I never had but everything I had in my lifetime: a good family, respect for learning, compassion for others, and some four-letter words for all occasions: words like help, give, care, feel, and love.[6]
—*Sam Levenson*

PART TWO
Loved Ones

CHAPTER 5

Launching Children

Big life transitions have three phases: the long goodbye . . .
the messy middle . . . and the new beginning.[1]
—*Bruce Feiler*

Introduction

THIS IS a bittersweet moment. As hands-on parents (partnered or single), we have served for years as loving guardians—providing, protecting, and nurturing. Now our children are grown and leaving the nest as they venture forth to college or graduate school, the work world, their own living space—perhaps, even, very far away from the home in which we raised them.

This ritual shows them that (as hard as it is to let go of them) you support them and gives you permission to feel, at least in part, happy that they are leaving—after all, they're doing what you raised them to do. This ritual honors everyone's new roles and celebrates these life changes.

Questions to Consider
- How does it feel to become a loving guide, rather than a guardian?
- Looking to the future, what new directions do you want your parental role to take?
- What emotional space do you feel the young person about to launch is in right now?

The Gathering

Time and Place

This gathering can occur at any time during the season when your children venture forth out of the nest. A particularly resonant time might be a Saturday evening around *Havdalah*. This ritual can happen in your home or any other place that might hold significance for you and your children.

People

Invite close friends and family to gather for this ritual. Tell those who will be attending that they will be invited to offer a personal blessing to the ones who are leaving home.

Materials

In advance, gather a few of your child's keepsakes, a box, and wrapping paper. You may also want to bring a gift or two, such as a mezuzah for their new home, items to have on hand when living in a new climate, and so forth.

Ritual

Begin by telling your children that the years you spent focused on parenting them were precious to you. Say:

> All the years of your life, I nurtured and sheltered you. From now on, I will be your guide rather than your guardian, ready to offer love and support as you face your future with courage and integrity. As you take the next steps in widening the frame of your world, I offer you this blessing:

> May all your learning lead to wisdom. May all your labors lead to success. May all your knowledge lead you to kindness. May the path before you lead to blessings. May your studies never cease. May all your prayers be answered. Amen.[2]

Share a few keepsakes from their early years growing up. Place those in a box, wrap up the box, and save the keepsakes for the next generations of family that may possibly come.

Acknowledge that this young adult will have different needs from you now, which you are willing to provide by offering some provision for their journey: a pair of new sneakers; a mezuzah; a tool kit filled with hammers, wrenches, screwdrivers; other items you feel they might need; and—depending on where they are moving—a snow shovel or a pair of flip-flops.

Parents say these blessings:

בָּרוּךְ שֶׁפְּטָרַנִי מֵעָנְשׁוֹ\מֵעָנְשָׁהּ שֶׁל זֹה.

Baruch shep'tarani mei-onsho/mei-onshah shel zoh.

The literal translation of this blessing is "Blessed is the One who has released me/exempted me from this one's punishment." In a traditional context, once a child becomes bet mitzvah, they are responsible in the eyes of God for the consequences of their own actions. In other words, "My job is done, thank God!"

בָּרוּךְ אַתָּה בְּבֹאֶךָ וּבָרוּךְ אַתָּה בְּצֵאתֶךָ.

Baruch atah b'vo-echa uvaruch atah b'tzeitecha.

You were blessed in your coming
and may you be blessed in your going.
—Deuteronomy 28:6, adapted

Next, invite those present to offer support and individual blessings.

Together, everyone recites or sings *T'filat HaDerech*, also known as the Traveler's Prayer:

>May you be blessed as you go on your way
>May you be guided in peace
>May you be blessed with health and joy
>May this be your blessing, amen.
>May you be sheltered by wings of peace
>May you be kept in safety and in love
>May grace and compassion find their way to every heart
>May this be your blessing, amen.
>Amen, may this be your blessing, amen.[3]

Dana and Chad's Story

"As our kids became adults, they started to be responsible for things we used to do for them. This shift has been emotional and monumental. Our three kids are different from each other, so launching them has varied depending on who they are as individuals and who we happened to be at each particular point. Our eldest, with whom we felt all those first highs and lows, now has her own apartment and a partner and they're thinking of getting married, and that feels new and strange. We used to worry that our middle child would miss his classes or be late for important events. Now we know that his way is often the long way, and we had to learn to back off. And our youngest likes to have a lot going on all the time, mostly takes care of what she needs to, and still turns to us for support. The challenge is remembering how much to be hands-on and how much to let them take over and do things themselves."

> I invited each of my kids out to dinner and, while we waited for dessert, handed them a credit card in their own name.
> —Rabbi Elaine Rose Glickman

Steve's Story

"Our kids' leaving was hard for me in the way that my identity as a dad is so central to who I am. I've figured out how to convert my 'dad time' around the dinner table, at the beach, or on drives to and from school and social events to focusing on where my involvement counts the most now—weekly conversations about college, life in a new city, and things like that. Not a day goes by in which I don't miss their energy and their presence, but my sense of loss has been mitigated by being able to travel and having the chance to relearn who it is that I married, because that really got lost in the long years of hands-on parenting."

For Clergy: Adapting for Communal Settings

Create a Friday night service celebrating graduating high school seniors with a blessing from the parents to their children. One example of a blessing:

Parents: We have watched you grow into who you are today. At this moment of a new beginning, we feel sadness and also joy. We have tried to instill in you the values of our people, in the hope that you will live your life with goodness and compassion. As you venture into the world, always remember that our love will never end, our support will never waver, and we will always be present for you when you need us. Now, as we send you off to your next chapter, may you take all that we have given you and make it part of who you are.

Graduates: I take with me all that you have given me—your love, your caring, your dreams for my life and hopes for my future. I accept the responsibility to live my life with the courage you have given me to be who I am and to honor the teachings of my heritage. As I go toward my future, I bring with me the love I feel for my family, knowing that in my heart you will always be with me. I am so proud to stand here with you tonight and to express my gratitude for your devotion to me and your willingness to send me off into the world. I look forward to my new adventure.

Clergy: May God bless you and protect you from harm and misfortune. May you have the strength to know that difficult times are a part of the fabric of life and that you have been blessed with friends and family to help you on your journey.

May God's face shine upon you and be gracious to you in guiding your way toward the future. May the light of knowledge help you to see your place in the world.

May you feel God's presence, and may you be granted peace of mind, of body, of soul. May you know that your life is somehow a part of all the other Jewish young people, who, like you and like our ancestors Abraham and Sarah, have ventured from their homes to find the answers to so many questions. Go, and take with you the truth of your connectedness to all of us here and to all human beings, all created with a spark of goodness, all created with divine light. May the light of the Divine shine upon you and through you, and illuminate your path.[4]

Words of Wisdom

Joy
The asters shake from stem to flower
waiting for the monarchs to alight.

Every butterfly knows that the end
is different from the beginning

and that it is always a part
of a longer story, in which we are always
transformed. When it's time to fly,
you know how, just the way you knew

how to breathe, just the way the air
knew to find its way into your lungs,

the way the geese know when to depart,
the way their wings know how to

speak to the wind, a partnership of feather
and glide, lifting into the blue dream.[5]

—*Stuart Kestenbaum*

CHAPTER 6

Relaunching Ourselves

Awaken your spirit to adventure;
Hold nothing back, learn to find ease in risk;
Soon you will be home in a new rhythm,
For your soul senses the world that awaits you.[1]
—*John O'Donohue*

Introduction

OUR TIME raising children was life-changing for us. And now that our roles with those children—now young adults—have changed, our relationship with ourselves, and with the world, is changing too. There might be a lot less laundry, less food in the refrigerator, no more tuition to pay, and more time to hang out with friends or take care of yourself. We're free to decide how and where we spend our time, with whom we choose to play and work, as well as to pursue what feels most meaningful to us now.

Questions to Consider

- What will you do with your newfound freedom?
- Who do you want to be (and be with) at this juncture in your life?
- What new commitments can you imagine making?

The Gathering

Time and Place

After your young adult children have left the nest (at least for the first time—they may still come back), there are moments when your new status feels particularly real. The gathering can take place in the family home or a friend's home or in a quiet private communal space, perhaps on a Saturday evening when havdalah is traditionally said. Alternatively, you can use these havdalah symbols and gather on a Sunday morning, a weeknight evening, or anytime the people important to you can join you.

People

Your chosen family and friends, including one—possibly a clergy member—who could serve as the ritual facilitator.

Materials

Havdalah candle and something to light it with
Spice bags
Wine cups/glasses
Wine or grape juice

Ritual

This ritual is designed for one parent and can be adapted for two.

The ritual facilitator holds up the *Havdalah* candle and says:

> This braided candle represents a weaving together of the different strands of your life. You are moving from a focus on active parenting to a new stage. Imagine the possibilities! Reading the Sunday *New York Times* in bed with your morning coffee; walking around your house wearing whatever you please; deciding at the last minute to meet friends for dinner.
>
> Now there is time to ask what brings you joy and purpose as you move forward and to experiment with dreams, hobbies, passions, and people you hadn't previously been able to pursue. What old friends are part of this new stage? What new friends will be part of the journey? What new light can illuminate the path ahead?

The ritual facilitator lights the candle and leads the group in the blessing:

בָּרוּךְ אַתָּה, יְיָ, אֱלֹהֵינוּ מֶלֶךְ הָעוֹלָם, בּוֹרֵא מְאוֹרֵי הָאֵשׁ.

Baruch atah, Adonai, Eloheinu Melech haolam, borei m'orei ha-eish.

Blessed are You, Source of life and all Creation—You create the fire's light.

Everyone present is invited to offer a blessing for the guest(s) of honor by filling in this sentence:

> As [name of person] move(s) toward their relaunching, I hope that [name] will bring their hard-earned [skill or quality] with them.

Ritual facilitator says:

These skills and qualities are the spices that our guest of honor is bringing with them moving forward. Let's recite the blessing over the spices:

בָּרוּךְ אַתָּה, יְיָ, אֱלֹהֵינוּ מֶלֶךְ הָעוֹלָם, בּוֹרֵא מִינֵי בְשָׂמִים.

Baruch atah, Adonai, Eloheinu Melech haolam, borei minei v'samim.

Blessed are You, Source of life and all Creation—
You create the varied spices.

Together, everyone recites or sings *T'filat HaDerech*, also known as the Traveler's Prayer:

May you be blessed as you go on your way
May you be guided in peace
May you be blessed with health and joy
May this be your blessing, amen.
May you be sheltered by wings of peace
May you be kept in safety and in love
May grace and compassion find their way to every heart
May this be your blessing, amen.
Amen, may this be your blessing, amen.[2]

The guest(s) of honor then shares three intentions of what might be a focus of this relaunching and how they might want this time ahead to feel.

In relaunching myself/ourselves, I/we will focus on:
I/we want this time ahead to feel:

Everyone raises a glass and recites the *Kiddush* blessing together:

בָּרוּךְ אַתָּה, יְיָ, אֱלֹהֵינוּ מֶלֶךְ הָעוֹלָם, בּוֹרֵא פְּרִי הַגָּפֶן.

Baruch atah, Adonai, Eloheinu Melech haolam, borei p'ri hagafen.

Blessed are You, Source of life and all Creation—
You create the fruit of the vine.

The guest (or guests) of honor extinguishes the *Havdalah* candle by turning it upside down in a half-filled wineglass.

Ritual facilitator says:

There is a traditional blessing that speaks about the work of Creation. In reciting it, we recognize and celebrate the opportunity for [guest(s) of honor] and all of us to renew ourselves.

וּבְטוּבוֹ מְחַדֵּשׁ בְּכָל יוֹם תָּמִיד מַעֲשֵׂה בְרֵאשִׁית.

Uvtuvo m'chadeish b'chol yom tamid maaseih v'reishit.

Who with goodness continually renews the work of Creation.

We close with the blessing for new beginnings, the *Shehecheyanu*. Everyone gathered recites:

בָּרוּךְ אַתָּה, יְיָ, אֱלֹהֵינוּ מֶלֶךְ הָעוֹלָם,
שֶׁהֶחֱיָנוּ וְקִיְּמָנוּ וְהִגִּיעָנוּ לַזְּמַן הַזֶּה.

*Baruch atah, Adonai, Eloheinu Melech haolam,
shehecheyanu v'kiy'manu v'higianu laz'man hazeh.*

Blessed are You, Source of life and all Creation—You have kept us in life, sustained us, and brought us to this moment of a new beginning.

Follow this with a great party.

Other ways to mark this moment:
* Celebrate by going on a trip to a place you always wanted to visit.
* Treat yourself and someone you love to a very special dinner at a restaurant of your choice.
* Go to Burning Man or follow the Dead & Company (or any other cultural adventure that makes you feel gloriously alive).

Cynthia's Story

"I went to NYU for film production, because I painted a lot as a kid and I thought that working in film was more practical than being 'a painter.' I had no idea what painters did. I met my husband in NYC, and after we both graduated and worked a number of jobs, we headed to the suburbs for a pretty house with a garden where we could raise a family. As soon as we enrolled our twins in kindergarten, I went back to school for a library science degree so that I could work as a librarian. And I had my group of mom friends—we all had this pool of kid and school knowledge in common. This whole time, I was still painting.

"Once the kids went to college I left the library job with the thought, 'Well, now I'll *really* paint.' Then I secured a job at a nearby university where the money was good, and possibilities opened, which led me to think, 'Maybe I'll go to grad school and really get my MFA like I've always wanted to do.' My boss promised to make the schedule work. In this program, I found a whole group of people who were interested in the same things. We had a common vocabulary and a way of playing with new ideas that has been very liberating. Just like the moms had this pool of knowledge that was mom-centered, the artists have this pool of knowledge that is art-centered. Being with them has reawakened me in ways that are not connected to my kids or my husband or my house. It's just who I am, that's it. I'm being my own self."

For Clergy: Adapting for Communal Settings

For individuals who are part of a Jewish family, this could be part of a communal *Havdalah* event with others in your community who are also marking this moment in their lives.

For those within families of other faiths, any of the above blessings can be incorporated into a religiously or spiritually significant service.

Words of Wisdom
The empty nest is underrated.[3]
—Nora Ephron

CHAPTER 7

Celebrating Friendship

Choni the Circle Maker was a Talmudic sage whose wisdom gave him the power to draw down rain for the community during periods of drought. According to one Rabbinic story, Honi fell into a deep sleep for seventy years. When he awoke, no one he knew was still alive and no one he met believed that he was really the legendary Circle Maker. In his distress, he prayed for mercy, and died. Rava said, "This explains the folk saying 'Either friendship or death,' as one who has no friends is better off dead."
—Based on Babylonian Talmud, Taanit 23a

Introduction

FRIENDSHIP is one of life's most magnificent gifts. Perhaps chief among them is the experience of being clearly seen by another person whom we like and trust and with whom we can share adventures. The Mishnah offers us some instruction on how to acquire for yourself a friend: "Get a companion to eat with, drink with, study with, sleep with, and reveal secrets, the secrets of the Torah and the secrets of worldly things" (*Avot D'Rabbi Natan* 8:3). In today's terms, this translates as: Go out for coffee a few times, then out to lunch; after a few lunches, try dinner or drinks. Then maybe study a Jewish text together or read the same book and talk about it. After a while, go off on a spa weekend or a wilderness trek, and finally you are ready (or already) sharing the secrets of your life and the secrets of the world.

Deep friendships can last through life's ups and downs, if circumstances allow and we treat them with care. But that isn't always possible. Sometimes a bond is broken for reasons beyond anyone's control. Sometimes we choose to let go of a toxic relationship. In this chapter we offer rituals and blessings for celebrating lifelong friendship, acknowledging the loss of a cherished friend, letting go of a toxic friendship, and welcoming a new friendship and the promise it holds.

Questions to Consider

- Some of our friendships are based on shared interests, some on mutual trust, and some on aspiring to bring out the best in the other person. How do you think about your friendships?
- John O'Donohue writes about a concept from the Buddhist tradition called the *Kalyana-mitra*, the "noble friend." Your *Kalyana-mitra* "will not accept pretension but will gently and very firmly confront you with your own blindness."[1] Which of your friendships contain this element?
- Which of your friendships are most important for you?
- Do you have younger and older friends as well as those in your age cohort? If not, how might you cultivate them?
- Are there people who were once friends whom you are now ready to let go of?

The Gathering

Time and Place

This gathering can take place at any time of day or evening, at a favorite restaurant or someone's home.

People

Invite a friend (this ritual can be adapted for more, if you have a friend group that wants to do this together).

Materials

A pair of small votive candles in candleholders and matches

A recording of a song or a photo of a piece of art from the time and place you first met and/or became friends (to be brought by each participant)

A recording of a song or a photo of a piece of art that is current (to be brought by each participant)

Ritual

Sit down together and settle in. One person says:

> Tradition explains that we light two candles for Shabbat to remind us of the two different words used in Torah for how to mark this

holy day: *shamor v'zachor*, "guard and remember." We have been given a precious gift and have sustained it and helped it to flourish by safeguarding it and remembering it.

Light the first candle, and ask each other, "How have we guarded this friendship?"

Share the music or art that you brought with you from the time and place you first met and became friends. Take turns sharing a memory of those early experiences.

Light the second candle. Ask each other, "How have we remembered the gift of this friendship?"

Then recite this prayer with an interpretative translation:

בָּרוּךְ אַתָּה, יְיָ, אֱלֹהֵינוּ מֶלֶךְ הָעוֹלָם, הַמֵּכִין מִצְעֲדֵי גָבֶר.

Baruch atah, Adonai, Eloheinu Melech haolam, hameichin mitzadei gaver.

Source of life and all Creation, we are grateful for the gift
of companions who accompany us on our journeys.

Raise a glass and share a meal. Maybe end the meal by taking a selfie.

Lynne's Story

"On a September day in 1974, I walked into my first graduate school class at University of Southern California (USC). Having come from a large midwestern public university, I dressed according to custom: T-shirt, cut-off jeans, and clogs. I hadn't realized that USC students preferred a much more preppy look—opting for Bobbie Brooks and dresses. You can imagine how relieved I was to find someone in class dressed very much like me—Vicki.

"Since then, our friendship has grown and flourished. We see ourselves as twins separated at birth. It's amazingly common for us to show up wearing nearly identical outfits. Our values, interests, senses of humor, and opinions are closely aligned. We both feel safe enough to share our 'least pretty' parts with each other, and we know we will be fully accepted. I see Vicki as my sounding board, moral compass, editor, and grammar consultant, among a variety of other roles.

> According to Jewish tradition, the Rabbis say that every blade of grass has its own angel who watches over it and says, "Grow!" (*B'reishit Rabbah* 10:6). Since new friendship is in many ways like a seedling, this blessing could be offered: May we tend to our new friendship as we would a young plant—protecting it, nourishing it, and giving it the conditions to thrive.

"We are approaching the fiftieth anniversary of our friendship and decided to honor this occasion by planning a series of special events throughout the year. This January, we celebrated at the Getty Center and the Huntington Gardens with high tea (and champagne!). To that, we're planning to add a walking food tour in Venice. We're still deciding on other events that will make up our 'Golden Jubilee' year."

Ken's Story

"I've kept my college friends throughout the years. We go away every year for a weekend. Sometimes it's camping, a concert, or a road trip. We've now been doing this for thirty years. Sometimes we talk about the big things, such as: Who has been the biggest influence on your life? What are the most important lessons you've learned? If this was to be our very last conversation, what would you want to say? What is a secret you've never told me?"

Letting Go of a Toxic Friendship

At this stage of our lives, we may discover that we want to be free of friendships that suck energy and create negativity. Toxic friendships include ones characterized by jealousy, competition, manipulation, and an absence of mutuality. It is not easy to let them go, particularly if the friendship was once nurturing, is long-standing, or is part of an ongoing social network. Perhaps the best strategy is to tell this friend that the friendship is difficult and no longer sustaining, but this is often too difficult. Another is simply to reduce contact. To give yourself the support you need to let this friend go, you might share this decision with one or two other friends, affirm your decision to let go of this relationship motivated primarily by obligation, and give more priority to taking care of yourself. That moment would be a quiet ritual and might include words like this poem by Robert Frost.

> *Nothing Gold Can Stay*
> Nature's first green is gold,
> Her hardest hue to hold.
> Her early leaf's a flower;
> But only so an hour.
> Then leaf subsides to leaf.
> So Eden sank to grief,
> So dawn goes down to day.
> Nothing gold can stay.[2]
> —*Robert Frost*

On Mourning a Friend

Regarding the loss of a friend, Rabbi Naamah Kelman writes: When we lose a friend in their young adult years, it is a shattering experience. It's not supposed to happen. We can spend decades wondering, what if? Who would they be? I remember standing at this young friend's grave after he was killed in an Israeli Air Force accident. My son was the exact same age. When this friend died, so did our sense of a carefree young adulthood. And yet we lived, and to this day he will always be twenty-three.

But as we enter our last decades, the loss of dear and lifelong friends is painful in other ways. The years of shared experiences, ups and downs, life's losses and blessings, create a bedrock of security and comfort. Who knows us better than that friend from youth, or that one from college, or that parent I met at our kids' preschool, or that fellow student who has become a lifelong colleague and friend? Research keeps telling us that deep friendships have the most positive effect on quality of life and even longevity. Our oldest friends are the great sources of our history, folly, and triumph. We know each other in ways that even our siblings, spouses, and children do not, and yet we often do not have a role in their funeral or any obligation for mourning.

But grieve and mourn we do and must.

When someone dies without children and little family, friends sometimes step in to oversee the funeral, even sit a symbolic shivah, and gather once a year for the *yahrzeit*. Here, friends act like family, and their grief is the public expression of this person's death. But in most situations, where the family handles all arrangements, how can we participate in the roles and rites when our beloved friends leave us? How do we comfort ourselves when we find ourselves losing more and more friends to infirmity, mental and physical? And what happens when children move their parents far away from their close friends so they can take care of them?

It behooves us to consider a number of rituals or acts of memorializing lost friends. Friendships are stories to be told, to be celebrated. When my young friend died, we friends spent an evening telling stories about him. We recorded it and gave it to the family. When my father passed away too early, his colleagues who were his friends put together a booklet of eulogies and reminisces for us, his children, for posterity.... Most friends will support the immediate family in their mourning but not necessarily have the space, time, or rituals to mourn the death themselves. Writing, recording, and videotaping is one way. The eulogy that you did not give at the funeral should be written and shared with other common friends, as well as family.

What about saying *Kaddish* (the Mourner's Prayer)? In liberal Jewish traditions, *Kaddish* can be said by friends as well as family. Or one can stand for *Kaddish* without saying it aloud as a way to mark the week, month, or year following the death. And just as the family has its own private mourning, a group of friends could certainly create some mourning time as well.

When people share friends, they can gather, perhaps for an evening of stories. How about an annual gathering of closest friends over lunch at that friend's favorite restaurant? Maybe visit some place you all loved, or listen to music you all enjoyed, or watch that movie that you all laughed so hard at or cried through together.

But what if you did not share friends? One of my dearest friends lost one of her dearest friends whom I knew only casually. But I knew my friend would need comforting; I knew she would need something to mark the loss. I treated her as if she were a first-degree mourner.

As we move into our later sixties, seventies, and even eighties, we can actually use this time to reclaim friendship. With children grown up and even grandchildren independent, we can turn back to dear and beloved friends, travel with them, dine with them, take in culture with them. It is a period to really savor friendships; this is how we bring meaning and comfort to our lives. Investing in friends at this time in our lives paradoxically eases the pain of loss. By creating new memories and relishing the past and hoping for the future together, we are not alone.

When we lose a life partner, siblings, or, God forbid, children, these are terrible losses; a part of us has been taken. Friends are different. We have hopefully worked out our "issues" and enjoyed their company and counsel. It is a loss but also a recognition of that wonderful aspect of ourselves that this particular friend was so able to help us see and know. In the death of our loved ones, we die a little bit. With friends, we are reminded of how we lived and formed our lives.

> Rhaina Cohen, author of *The Other Significant Others*, describes a sixth-century ritual between two monks from Syria. Before they left their Jordanian monastery to become desert hermits together, the abbot knelt with each man on either side and prayed for them. The ritual between these two men was the inaugural act of *adelphopoiesis*, literally "the making of brothers." For centuries in the East, these rituals took place in Christian churches.[4]

Friendships are unique; there's that bird-watching friend, or that crazy childhood friend, or that colleague who seemed so different; or that woman whom you saved after her divorce and you became soul sisters. Friends express different aspects of ourselves and different biographies and periods in our lives. We need to figure out how we might mourn, let go, and ultimately celebrate what sustained us.

This is an invitation to do so . . .[3]

For Clergy: Adapting for Communal Settings

Different ways to mark friendships include:

- ❧ Honor *chavurot* in the community by dedicating a Shabbat service and inviting the *chavurot*. It might include a blessing from the clergy such as the following:

  > Our tradition teaches us in *Pirkei Avot*, "Make for yourself a teacher, acquire for yourself a friend, and give each person the benefit of the doubt" (1:6). Another teaching asks how one acquires a friend. The answer: Get a companion to eat with, drink with, study with, celebrate with, raise kids together, share joy together, be present to each other through the losses and celebrations of your lives . . . Your *chavurah* has been doing this for [number] years; you have become a chosen family. You began all those years ago joining a group of people you might not have known, deciding in advance that you would find what was special about each other instead of being critical and judgmental. And now, as you look back over those years, you see how grateful you are for the deep friendships you have formed and for the many memories you have of the journey you have taken together and the hope that the friendships you have created continue into the journey that lies ahead.

- ❧ Invite two friends who have studied sacred texts together to give a teaching.
- ❧ When someone has lost a friend, encourage them to share some reflections about their friend before *Kaddish*.

Words of Wisdom

At its core, life is not about things, it is about relationships. It is the hands we go on holding in our hearts at the end that define the kind of life we have led.[5]

—*Sister Joan Chittister*

CHAPTER 8
Renewimg Partnership Vows

Once the realization is accepted that even between the closest people there remain infinite distances, a wonderful coexistence can develop once they succeed in loving the vastness between them that affords them the possibility of seeing each other in their full gestalt before a vast sky.[1]
—*Rainer Maria Rilke*

Introduction

YOU ARE APPROACHING a major anniversary. One long marriage. But in fact, within your marriage there are many marriages. There is the honeymoon marriage: new, romantic, passionate, and crucial for creating a foundation for a life together. In fact, the importance of this stage is acknowledged in Torah with the prohibition of conscripting a recently married man into the army for a year after his wedding "to give happiness to the woman he has married" (Deuteronomy 24:5). After a while, the real world begins to intervene, with pressures like work or child care or homemaking or the complications that come with in-laws. You begin to notice more acutely the ways in which your partner is not perfect—and maybe even irritating some of the time. Hence the expression "The honeymoon is over!" After more time, some partners may begin to wonder if there is someone better out there. This stage is often called "the seven-year itch." If your marriage survives past these temptations, it might develop into a growing-together stage as both spouses have become more mature, careers more settled, children (if you have them) growing up and perhaps getting ready to leave the nest. Now there is more time to be together, to focus on each other. Still, there are challenges as each partner ages. With growing older sometimes come physical and emotional changes. For some, this is the stage where the couple is dealing with frail parents, illness, and concern about an impending retirement. None of this is easy to manage, but for those couples who work through these challenges, there emerges a sense of fulfillment that they have weathered so many storms together and gratitude that they have each other. Some describe this phase as falling in love all over again.

Not all marriages follow this pattern, but you might recognize your own as having some of these stages. As a major anniversary beckons, you want to celebrate wherever you are in your relationship. Alternatively, perhaps you've been through a tough time together and want to celebrate that you are still together and still looking forward. You want to renew the vows you made years ago with each other in the presence of people you love and who have been part of your lives up to this point. You want to look back over your journey, recommit to each other, and affirm that you will continue to be together in whatever challenges and joys might lie ahead.

You also might want to honor some of the people who have brought blessings to your life together, and so you invite them in advance to be prepared to offer you (very brief) blessings in their own words.

Questions to Consider
- Why have you decided to renew your vows?
- Do you want to acknowledge the past or to embrace the future? Or both?
- From whom would you welcome blessings?

The Gathering

Time and Place

Select a date on or near a major anniversary at your home, the location where you were married, or a place that you love—a park, a restaurant, a friend's home.

People

Invite family and friends, and an officiant/clergy/friend who will serve as ritual facilitator.

Materials

- A marriage canopy (chuppah)
- A cup, ideally one that has some meaning, such as the cup you might have used at your wedding, one that belonged to a

parent, one you use at home for religious observance, a college mug, or a new cup you have bought for this occasion
A glass to be broken
A new covenant (vows) that you have written
Objects representing stages of your lives
A bag or a container to hold those objects
Wine or grape juice
Rings (or gifts)

Ritual

The couple walks to the marriage canopy together or accompanied by children or grandchildren. If they choose to circle each other, the ritual facilitator might say:

> Three circles; three Biblical verses: I will betroth you to me forever; I will betroth you in righteousness, in justice, in loving-kindness and compassion, and I will betroth you to me in faithfulness. (Hosea 2:21–22)

Officiant continues:

> You spoke vows to each other [number] years ago.
> Now, [number] years later, you renew those vows,
>   this time with more awareness and intention.
> I invite you to renew those vows now.

The couple then reads their individual vows or their original marriage contract (*ketubah*) aloud, if they had one. Then the couple exchanges rings (or perhaps some other gift) with these words:

> הֲרֵי אֲנִי מְחַדֵּשׁ\מְחַדֶּשֶׁת אֶת בְּרִית הַנִּשּׂוּאִין
> בֵּינֵינוּ בְּטַבַּעַת זוֹ\בְּמַתָּנָה זוֹ.
> *Harei ani m'chadeish/m'chadeshet et b'rit hanisuin*
> *beineinu b'tabaat zo/b'matanah zo.*

> With this ring/gift, I renew our loving covenant of marriage.

Officiant:

> [Number] years ago, seven blessings might have been chanted at your wedding over a cup of wine. One of them may have included these words:

שַׂמֵּחַ תְּשַׂמַּח רֵעִים הָאֲהוּבִים,
כְּשַׂמֵּחֲךָ יְצִירְךָ בְּגַן עֵדֶן מִקֶּדֶם.
Samei-ach t'samach rei-im haahuvim
k'sameichacha y'tzircha b'gan Eiden mikedem.

May these loving companions rejoice together with the joy
You have set aside for them since Adam and Eve
rejoiced in the Garden of Eden *mikedem*.

What does *mikedem* mean? Sometimes it is translated as "as of old," which means the blessing could be translated as "May you rejoice . . . as Adam and Eve did in the days of old in the Garden of Eden." But there is another translation, a deeper one. *Kedem* comes from the same root as "east," as in east of Eden. With that understanding, the blessing becomes: "May you rejoice east of the Garden of Eden." And where is east of Eden?

Right here, where we all live.

[Partner one] and [Partner two], you don't live in that primordial Garden of Eden. None of us do. You live in the real world. And it is in this real world that you have made a life together, (raised a family,) and made a difference in the world. Together you have created a garden with your love and enabled it to grow—your own Garden of Eden.

So now we offer you seven new blessings, spoken over a cup of wine in the cup that [explain the significance of the cup].

Invite seven people to offer creative blessings in categories such as health, friendship, love, creativity, wisdom, humor, and tolerance—or choose your own categories. Alternatively, invite seven family members or friends from different stages of your lives to offer blessings. These could be someone who knew one or both of you as you were growing up, someone from college, someone from the time you got married or from the early days of building your career, someone from when your kids (if you have them) were little, or someone with whom you have traveled, worked on a volunteer project, or shared a hobby. You might decide to invite one or all of your adult children or young people from your chosen family for a final blessing.

Once these seven blessings are over, conclude with the blessing over the wine:

בָּרוּךְ אַתָּה, יְיָ, אֱלֹהֵינוּ מֶלֶךְ הָעוֹלָם, בּוֹרֵא פְּרִי הַגָּפֶן.

Baruch atah, Adonai, Eloheinu Melech haolam, borei p'ri hagafen.

Blessed are You, Source of life and all Creation—
You create the fruit of the vine.

The couple, and perhaps additional family members, share that cup.

Officiant offers a blessing, perhaps the traditional Priestly Blessing, with the following interpretive translation:

יְבָרֶכְךָ יְיָ וְיִשְׁמְרֶךָ.
יָאֵר יְיָ פָּנָיו אֵלֶיךָ וִיחֻנֶּךָּ.
יִשָּׂא יְיָ פָּנָיו אֵלֶיךָ
וְיָשֵׂם לְךָ שָׁלוֹם.

Y'varech'cha Adonai v'yishm'recha.
Ya-eir Adonai panav eilecha vichuneka.
Yisa Adonai panav eilecha
v'yaseim l'cha shalom.

May the Divine Presence bless you and protect you.
May the light of the Divine shine upon you and through you
and illuminate your path.
May you see the face of the Divine in the face of every human being
and so experience wholeness and peace.

Break a glass. Follow with a fabulous party!

New Approaches to Jewish Wedding Customs

Some customs from Jewish traditions connected to marriage might be reimagined in a renewal ceremony:

1. Chuppah: The chuppah is a temporary canopy that symbolizes a home—fragile, but safe; open on all sides to family and friends, but closed on top to remind the partners that their connection to each other is intimate and different from all other relationships. You might want to use the chuppah that was originally used at your wedding or some cloth that has

become meaningful to you over your years together. You could also create a new chuppah with the help of family and friends or commission one that you donate to a synagogue in gratitude for this ceremony.

2. Circling: In some Jewish weddings, one partner circles the other seven times, symbolizing the mystical notion that there are seven layers to a person's soul, and the circling represents connecting on each of these levels and creating a sacred and protected space for the beloved's soul. Sometimes each partner circles the other three times, and they conclude with a seventh circling, which they do together like a dance. Others adapt this custom to three circles (one each with the third together) with the verses from the prophet Hosea (included in the ritual above).

3. Breaking a glass: A glass is often broken at the end of a Jewish wedding. There are many different explanations for this tradition, including that it recalls the destruction of the ancient Temples in Jerusalem and reminds the couple that the world we live in is broken and in need of repair. Another explanation is that the broken glass punctuates the ceremony with the assurance that although the path ahead will include sorrow as well as joy, the first steps taken after a wedding are taken through that brokenness with the conviction that love can be a force for healing.

Isa and Bill's Story

"During the span of fifty years, we've been married twice—to each other. The first marriage was when we were graduate students together; I was studying education, and Bill was studying sociology. We moved to California for Bill's job while I worked on my doctorate. Four years later we moved to Los Angeles for my job as a museum educator. By then, Bill had changed careers and was a freelance photographer as I became a professor of education. We had our kids in California, raised them, and are now grandparents. Part of why we wanted a rewedding was that our first wedding ceremony was planned by the rabbis of the synagogue where my family belonged; it didn't really reflect either of us. We wanted a rewedding that we would create together, that reflected who we are and would celebrate how we had grown and changed throughout our life together. We wanted it to be intimate, just really close friends and family in our backyard. Bill built a chuppah with the involvement of our four-year-old grandson. We invited friends from different stages in our lives to offer us blessings. After each friend spoke, we described an artifact from that time, explained its significance, and placed it in a Native American basket that we and our adult children had selected for this purpose on a recent family trip. The artifacts included a small camera, some significant family photographs, and an article Bill and I had written together. As we placed the artifacts in the basket we made promises to each other. Then our kids and their spouses blessed us. Bill broke the glass to shouts of '*Mazal Tov!*'"

For Clergy: Adapting for Communal Settings
Couples can celebrate their recommitment by receiving a blessing from their clergyperson in their place of worship or by planning a rewedding ceremony together:

Our God and God of our ancestors, bless this couple [or: these couples] on this, the anniversary of their marriage.

May you reflect with deep gratitude upon the years that have passed. Many and varied have been your experiences since that moment. May you recall the joys that have sweetened your lives; may you be thankful for the strength that allowed you to weather the storms that shook you to your very roots.

God, You have been with this couple through all their years together; so may You continue to bless them with Your presence in the years to come.[2]

> **The Longlyweds Know**
> That it isn't about the Golden Anniversary at all,
> But about all the unremarkable years
> that Hallmark doesn't even make a card for.
>
> It's about the 2nd anniversary when they were surprised
> to find they cared for each other more than last year
>
> And the 4th when both kids had chickenpox
> and she threw her shoe at him for no real reason
>
> And the 6th when he accidentally got drunk on the way
> home from work because being a husband and father
> was so damn hard
>
> It's about the 11th and 12th and 13th years when
> they discovered they could survive crisis
>
> And the 22nd anniversary when they looked
> at each other across the empty nest, and found it good.
>
> It's about the 37th year when she finally
> decided she could never change him
>
> And the 38th when he decided
> a little change wasn't that bad
>
> It's about the 46th anniversary when they both
> bought cards, and forgot to give them to each other
>
> But most of all it's about the end of the 49th year
> when they discovered you don't have to be old
>
> to have your 50th anniversary!!!![3]
> —Leah Furnas

Words of Wisdom

Your partner gives you the greatest gift of your adult life: the choice to be your companion and to walk with you through all of life's fluctuations. Every day, remember to thank each other and to offer at least one appreciation. This very simple act will infuse your shared life with positive energy and a generosity of spirit for the journey ahead.[4]

—Judith Ansara and Robert Gass

CHAPTER 9

Becoming a Grandparent/Grandfriend

A grandparent's light—whether it shines only briefly or for many years—can illuminate a family's path for generations to come.[1]
—Jerry Witkovsky and Deanna Shoss

Introduction

WE'VE PROBABLY ALL HEARD some of the classic jokes about being a grandparent. One, attributed to Sam Levenson, is well-known: "The reason grandchildren and grandparents get along so well is that they have a common enemy." We've also probably become aware of the *five-minute rule* when we spend time with friends: No more than five minutes of any gathering should include the sharing of pictures of grandchildren. Why? Because not everyone has children or grandchildren, and some who do don't have the kind of relationship with them that they wish they had. As we imagine ceremonies for becoming a grandparent, we want to include grandfriends, the intentional intergenerational connection between an older person and a child that is not part of a traditional family but rather a family of choice. We also want to acknowledge some of the challenges of grandparenting when there has been a divorce.

There are many moments worth marking in the ongoing connection between grandparents/grandfriends and their grandkids—the moment you know you have become a grandparent/grandfriend, which is different if you are living close by or if you live far away; the moment when you first hold that infant; or the moment of a baby naming or christening, a bet mitzvah, a quinceañera, a wedding. These moments are so different that we have collected different blessings as well as the ritual here, which was adapted from "Celebrating Grandparenthood," created by Mayyim Hayyim for the Jewish Grandparents Network.[2] We invite you to use or adapt this ritual in a way that works for you. We also hope you will to find a way to incorporate a version of one of the blessings below into one of these moments, instead of following a more scripted ritual. Whichever moment you choose to mark in whatever circumstance, this ceremony calls attention to the connection that can exist between generations, which is often so important both to those who are younger and those who are older.

The central element in this ritual is water. Water is a symbol for Creation: "God said: Let there be an expanse in the midst of the water, and let it divide water from water" (Genesis 1:6). Noah's ark floats on water, ensuring the continuation of all of Creation. Moses is rescued on a river. The Reed Sea parts as the Israelites escape to freedom. Miriam's well sustains the Israelites as they wander through the wilderness. Abraham (and Sarah) washed the feet of their (angelic) guests. Rebekah and Rachel are discovered at a well. Tradition teaches that just as one can't survive three days without water, one can't survive three days without Torah—hence the tradition of reading Torah three days a week. We pray for rain and dew in their appropriate seasons. The root for the word that means blessing (*b'rachah*) is the same root as the word for pool of water (*b'reichah*). Before we wash our hands, we say a blessing. The shape of water is always changing. As Heraclitus taught, one can never step in the same river twice; the river is always changing, as is the one who steps in. When you become a grandparent/grandfriend, you are part of that river, and you are also the one who steps in as you become an older generation.

Questions to Consider

- What are some of your feelings about becoming a grandparent/grandfriend?
- Was there a grandparent/grandfriend in your life who was important to you, and how?
- Is this moment different if the child is not present from a moment when the child and their parents and you can celebrate together?
- Is this a moment for you to be blessed or for you to bless this grandchild, or for both?

What do you want to be called? Popular options include saba, savta, oma, opa, nana, nonnie, papa, grandma, grandpa, bubbe, and zaydie. In Norway it's bestemor (best grandmother), bestefar (best grandfather), mormor (mother of my mother), farmor (father of my mother), morfar (mother of my father), and farfar (father of my father). A friend tells a story about how a woman she knew wanted to be called simply Grandma, but her eldest grandchild burst out with "Mike," and she was "Mike" forever after. It turns out that often it is the grandchild who chooses the name simply because that is what they can pronounce! That moment when you first hear the name you'll be called might be a moment for a *Shehecheyanu*.

Another variation on the ways people become grandparents/grandfriends is through becoming connected with a new partner who brings grandchildren or grandfriends into the mix. Often those children are older and perhaps less interested in spending time with the new grandparent/grandfriend. Here we share the advice of Laura's friend Sylvia Price, who recoupled in her seventies: "Remember your partner's grandchildren's birthdays, show up at events when appropriate, and be involved in their lives only when invited."

The Gathering

Time and Place

Host this ritual when a new baby/young child enters your life, at your home or the home of a close family member or friend.

People

Gather grandparent(s)/grandfriend(s), family and friends, and parents of the new baby if possible.

Materials

Wine cup (perhaps one that had been used at a child's [or a special friend's] wedding)
Wine or grape juice
A large bowl, ideally one that has some meaning to you

Ritual

Water-Pouring Ceremony[3]

FIRST POUR

Grandparent(s) says:

עֲטֶרֶת זְקֵנִים בְּנֵי בָנִים וְתִפְאֶרֶת בָּנִים אֲבוֹתָם.

Ateret z'keinim b'nei vanim, v'tiferet banim avotam.

Grandchildren are the crown of their elders.
Parents are the light to their children. (Proverbs 17:6)

I honor the stage of my life where I now hold [or, if this is not the first grandchild: again hold] the title of grandparent. As I pour water into this vessel, I affirm and celebrate the transition to grandparenthood. May I continue to discover new parts of myself and deepen my relationship with my children and grandchild[ren].

Next, the grandparent pours about a third of the water from the cup into the bowl.

SECOND POUR

Grandparent(s) says:

Here I am, having become a grandparent, knowing I have created a full life for myself, knowing that I have a circle of loved and loving ones who continue to celebrate this life stage with me, knowing that I am sheltered beneath the wings of a Divine Presence.[4]

מוֹדִים אֲנַחְנוּ לָךְ.

Modim anachnu lach.

I thank the Abundance of the universe for the good I know,
for the life I have, and for the gifts that are my daily portion:
For health and healing,
For the ever-renewed beauty of earth and sky,
For thoughts of truth and justice,
Which stir us from our ease
and move us to acts of goodness.[5]

I pour *mayim chayim*, living waters, to recognize the abundant gifts in my life, and the gift of being a grandparent.

The grandparent pours some more water into the bowl.

THIRD POUR

Grandparent(s) says:

> May the blessings and lessons of my experiences guide and sustain me as a grandparent.[6] May I be a nonjudgmental presence to my children, as they may parent differently from the way I did. May I love my grandchildren in the way they need to be loved, and may I be a safe and embracing presence for my family throughout their lives.
>
> I pour *mayim chayim*, living waters, in recognition of *l'dor vador* (from generation to generation). I honor my ancestors who came before me, and I take my place in this legacy.

The grandparent now pours the remainder of the water into the bowl.

Those present offer a blessing to the new grandparents/grandfriends.

After the ceremony, you may wish to use the water in the bowl to water plants around your home (or offer to pets) as an affirmation of the chain of life that is interconnected.

> In the Torah there are many examples of parents blessing children, but only one of a grandparent blessing grandchildren. Joseph brings his two sons, Ephraim and Manasseh, to meet Jacob. With his hands on their heads, Jacob says, "In the future, Israel will use you as a blessing. They will say, 'May God make you like Ephraim and Manasseh'" (Genesis 48:20). This is the basis for the traditional blessing that some Jews use to bless their sons on Shabbat evening. From this custom, there evolved a different blessing for daughters: "May you be like Sarah, Rebekah, Rachel, and Leah." The contemporary liturgist Marcia Falk offers an alternative parental blessing: "Be who you are and may you be blessed in all that you are."[7]

Additional Blessings

Blessing for a Grandchild

[Name of grandchild], as you are wrapped in your parents' arms, so may your life be wrapped in justice and righteousness. As we embrace you today, so may you embrace your traditions and your communities. As your eyes are filled with wonder when you gaze at the world, so too may you be filled with wonder at the everyday miracles of life. As you startle to the world around you, so may you remain ever open both to the happiness and to the pain of those you encounter in the world. As you cry for food and comfort now, so may you one day cry out to correct the injustices of the world, to help clothe the naked and feed the hungry. As your hand tightly grasps your parents' fingers, so may you grasp hold of learning to grow in knowledge and wisdom.[8]

Blessing for a New Grandparent/Grandfriend

Friends might say:

We joyously celebrate with you [name] as you become grandparent(s)/grandfriend(s) to this (little) one. May you be a loving presence in [name of child's] life, ready to cheer for their accomplishments and support them in their challenges. Every child needs a champion. May you be that champion for your grandchild/grandfriend. May you support their parent(s) as they raise their child(ren), ready with advice if they ask for it and a nonjudgmental presence when they don't. May your relationship with this (little) one animate your own sense of joy, adventure, curiosity, and love. May the wisdom that comes from your life experience become a part of this (little) one's life and memory, with you both learning from and teaching each other. Generations with generations—you are each part of the great circle of life.

Laura's Story

"When my son Joshua was young, he had an imaginary friend named Junger. When I would put him to bed, he would ask for a Junger story, one in which Junger had different superpowers that enabled him to take Joshua on magical adventures that usually involved fighting crime or unraveling mysteries. I made them up as I told them, and he seemed to love them. As he grew up, the Junger stories gave way to video games that were much more exciting, so the stories stopped. They began again when Joshua's son Avery was about four. When I babysat, I would tell Joshua's son about his father's invisible friend Junger. The ritual of those bedtime stories reconnected me to the little boy my son once was and created some wonderful memories with my grandson."

Craig's Story

"I love PJ Library, a program whose mission is to help families to connect with Jewish values, traditions, and culture whether or not they are engaged in the Jewish community in any other way. Once parents sign up, the child receives a high-quality children's book in the mail every month. It can begin as soon as a child is born and continues with age-appropriate books until the child is about twelve. For many of these children, that package addressed to the child is the only piece of mail they get that isn't from Amazon, and when it arrives it is exciting. The child feels important and seen. And it is completely free. While only parents can initiate the connection, the arrival of these books can be an opportunity for a grandparenting ritual—reading your grandchild a Jewish book. I started reading my granddaughter these books when she was a baby. And each time I opened the new one I said the *Shehecheyanu*, the prayer of gratitude to the Creator of life for bringing us to this moment. She's older now, and she sometimes reads to me. We always begin a new book with the *Shehecheyanu*."

Carol's Story

"Blended families take on additional dimensions when they are interfaith and are dedicated to bringing children together respectfully and meaningfully. My son raised his two children in a Jewish home with synagogue involvement and home celebration. He embarked on his new relationship with a caring Christian woman, who has three children, right at the time of his son's bar mitzvah. By the time of his daughter's bat mitzvah, the two families were one. At my granddaughter's bat mitzvah, all five children participated in the service. At home, they share all the holidays.

All the children, who are now young adults, call us Grandma and Grandpa. My daughter-in-law's daughter is expecting a baby girl, and her mother hosted a baby shower. Along with a gift, I wanted to create a special connection through a shared blessing for the little one. I wanted to offer a prayer that was respectful of their beliefs but also came authentically from me. I asked my sister to calligraph a version of the Shabbat evening prayer for a daughter: 'To our great-granddaughter: May the Holy One make you like Sarah, Rebekah, Rachel, and Leah. May the Holy One bless you and keep you. May the Holy One shine light upon you and be gracious to you. May the Holy One turn toward you and give you peace.' Coincidentally, at the shower there was a display board asking family and friends to write down their prayers for the baby. Clearly, we share love and respect through this sacred moment."

For Clergy: Adapting for Communal Settings

Invite all new grandparents/grandfriends to be honored in front of the community once a year for a special blessing. In Jewish or other faith communities, the timing might be connected with the Torah portion *Va-y'chi*, in which Jacob blesses his grandchildren.

Another option could take place during a grandchild/grandfriend's bet mitzvah. In the spirit of the Talmudic teaching "For whoever hears the *parashah* from their grandchild it is as if they heard it directly from Mount Sinai" (Jerusalem Talmud, *Shabbat* 1:2), invite grandparents/grandfriends to be part of a Torah passing from generation to generation.

You may also include a special grandparent prayer such as this one:

> God, we ask that You bless [name of grandchild]
> at this moment of holiness.
> Being here to celebrate this [bar mitzvah/bat mitzvah/bet mitzvah] day with you,
> our beloved [grandson/granddaughter/grandchild],
> fills us with a wonderful sense of joy.
> Called to Torah today,

may you continue to live a life
filled with the performance of mitzvot.
May you always be a source of pride and joy for us,
for your parents,
for the entire Jewish people.
Together we say: *Amen*.[9]

Words of Wisdom
One thing I know for certain: We are what survives us.[10]

—*Marc Freedman*

CHAPTER 10

Finalizing a Divorce or Separation

> When a man divorces the wife of his youth,
> even the altar of God sheds tears.
> —*Babylonian Talmud,* Gittin 90b

Introduction

IN MOST DIVORCES (or separations after a long-term relationship) God is not the only one to shed tears.[1] Divorce is more than the end of a marriage; it is also the acknowledgment of dreams that didn't come true. Divorce and separations are a kind of death that must be mourned before the individuals can go on to create new dreams.

A bit of background about divorce in Jewish tradition: According to Torah, only a husband can initiate a divorce, and he can do it for almost any reason. Over the centuries, Jewish religious courts assumed the right to compel a husband to divorce his wife in certain situations, but there remains the severe problem of the *agunah*, a woman whose husband refuses to grant her a divorce even though they are no longer living as husband and wife. Jewish law deems that a married woman must have a *get*, a divorce document, before she can remarry. It is not possible to obtain a *get* until after a civil divorce has taken place.

While many Jewish couples honor the tradition that requires a *get*, many others do not. It feels too patriarchal, too hierarchical, too impersonal. For those people, something else needs to be created—an alternative or egalitarian ritual that sees both partners as agents, as opposed to the woman as object. Since this moment marks a kind of death, the timing of the ceremony might be modeled after an unveiling, which usually takes place around a year after the burial when the headstone is unveiled. The unveiling reveals the headstone but, even more importantly, signals to the mourner and the community that the mourner is ready to "go forth in peace to life." After a funeral, the friends bring food and take care of the mourner. After an unveiling, the mourner's status changes; now they can feed those who took care of them. By imagining this ritual as a kind of unveiling, the divorced person signals a shift from what was most likely a dark and difficult time to a moment of celebration.

Questions to Consider

- Who are your witnesses, those people whom you want present at this ritual of ending?
- Where do you want it to take place?
- When do you want to do it?

The Gathering

Time and Place

This ritual should occur after the civil divorce is finalized, if you were legally married, in your home or the home of a friend.

People

Invite friends closest to you, especially those who supported you emotionally during the divorce process.

Materials

A candle for each participant
Matches
An alternate *get* document (example on page 79)
A planter with soil or an outdoor garden
A glass to be broken

Ritual

Place the unlit candles in a circle in front of each seat. Instruct the participants in advance to come prepared to share a brief story about a personal journey from darkness to light. After each individual shares their story, they light their candle.

The guest of honor reads the alternative *get* document. Each participant signs it.

The guest of honor steps on a glass, indicating that they are ready to move forward in their life. If in a place with a garden, go outdoors and bury the *get*. If not, bury the *get* in a planter's pot. Invite participants to offer a brief wish for what the guest of honor might want to bury from their marriage or relationship, as well as a short blessing for the next stage of their life.

All sing the *Shehecheyanu*:

בָּרוּךְ אַתָּה, יְיָ, אֱלֹהֵינוּ מֶלֶךְ הָעוֹלָם,
שֶׁהֶחֱיָנוּ וְקִיְּמָנוּ וְהִגִּיעָנוּ לַזְּמַן הַזֶּה.

*Baruch atah, Adonai, Eloheinu Melech haolam,
shehecheyanu v'kiy'manu v'higianu laz'man hazeh.*
Blessed are You, Source of life and all Creation—
You have kept us in life, sustained us, and brought us
to this moment of a new beginning.

Conclude with a meal served by the guest of honor.

Laura's Story

"As a feminist and a rabbi, I had worked over the years with many individuals who were going through divorce or separation. I thought I understood their pain, their shame, their anger, and their grief. I had often seen that civil divorce wasn't sufficient to help people separate emotionally as well as financially and physically. I had seen that for couples not legally married, the separation often went unmarked and therefore un-mourned in the context of community. It was an ambiguous loss. I thought I understood the need for Jewish ritual to help them move through their loss to a place where they could begin again. I thought I understood it all, but it wasn't until my own marriage ended after twelve years, two children, and a thousand shattered dreams that I really began to understand.

"I know full well that a traditional *get* is a patriarchal ritual in which a man releases his wife and his wife is released. Therefore, I was surprised to realize that I wanted a *get*. I understood the political reasons that a liberal Jew might choose an Orthodox *get*—so that no one could ever question the status of any children who might come in a second marriage.[2] But I was already forty; there was little chance of other children. So for me, the reasons to choose an Orthodox *get* were not political. They were personal. I felt I needed to be released, to be set free from the commitments and the promises I had made to this marriage and to the man I had loved since I was twenty years old. Somehow, I knew that this patriarchal ritual would be a step on the journey to a new beginning.

"Soon after my traditional *get*, eleven women friends joined me at my home to help me create a new ceremony. It was the fifth night of Chanukah. We began in darkness, sitting in a circle around the *chanukiyah* [Chanukah menorah]. I had asked each woman to come prepared to share a story about a journey from darkness to light. After each had shared her story, I thanked them all for helping me move from darkness to light. Then we lit the *chanukiyah* and sang the *Shehecheyanu*: 'Thank You, God, for having kept us in life, sustained us, and brought us to this time.' I read a new version of the *get*, one that I had written, where I was the subject rather than the object. After I read it aloud, all of my friends signed it as witnesses.

"Then we went into the backyard and stood near the trees I had planted at the covenant ceremonies of my son and daughter. Just as I had planted my son's foreskin and my daughter's umbilical cord, so we planted my version of the *get* under a new tree that my friends had given me as a present. As we buried it, I asked each of my friends to voice something they hoped I would bury from my marriage and divorce.

"We returned to the house, and I served the best dinner I could cook. After all the months of their feeding and caring for me, I was finally ready to give something back. I placed a present at each table setting to thank each of them for all their gifts of love. We ended the evening with singing, laughing, and some tears."

A Traditional *Get*

On the [*number*] day of the week, the [*Hebrew date*] day of the month of [*Hebrew month*] in the year [*Jewish year*] after creation of the world, according to the calendric calculations that we count here, in the city [*name of city*], which is situated on the [*name of nearby river*] river, and situated near springs of water, I, [*name of former husband*] the son of [*name of former husband's father*], who today am present in the city [*name of city*], which is situated on the [*name of nearby river*] river, and situated near springs of water, willingly consent, being under no duress, to release, discharge, and divorce you [to be] on your own, you, my wife [*name of former wife*] daughter of [*name of former wife's father*], who are today in the city of [*name of city*], which is situated on the [*name of nearby river*] river, and situated near springs of water, who has hitherto been my wife. And now I do release, discharge, and divorce you [to be] on your own, so that you are permitted and have authority over yourself to go and marry any man you desire. No person may object against you from this day onward, and you are permitted to every man. This shall be for you from me a bill of dismissal, a letter of release, and a document of absolution, in accordance with the law of Moses and Israel.

An Alternative *Get*

On the [*number*] day of the week, the [*Hebrew date*] day of the month of [*Hebrew month*] in the year [Jewish year] after the creation of the world, according to the calendric calculations that we count here, in the city [*name of city*], which corresponds to [*Gregorian date*], I, [*name*], who today am present in the city [*name of city*], willingly consent, being under no duress, to release, discharge, and divorce (or separate from) you to be on your own, you, my partner [*name of former partner*]. And now I do release, discharge, and divorce (or separate from) you to be on your own, so that you have authority over yourself to go and become a partner with anyone you desire or choose to not enter into a new partnership. This shall be a bill of dismissal, a letter of release, and a document of absolution, in accordance with the spirit of the law of Moses and the Jewish people.

Alternative Ways to Mark a Divorce

- Choose to wear a different kind of ring, like the divorce ring created out of your engagement and weddings rings.[3]
- Participate in a retreat geared toward navigating the multifaceted challenges of divorce or the end of a long-term relationship.[4]

Noam's Story

"I scream curses into a pillow until my lungs are empty and my eyes are full of tears. I am teetering between sadness and rage as I keep thinking about one word: divorce. Luckily, in my men's group, I'm in a room full of brothers who have been in difficult places before. They all hear and see me as more than just a broken mess of emotions. And they understand all the questions that run through my mind once my breath returns: What will I do? Where am I going to live? Are the kids going to be okay? What is co-parenting anyway? How much is this going to cost? What kind of rabbi am I if I let my marriage fail? My brothers see me grieving. They know that I am mourning a loss. Divorce is a death, but not like when someone dies. It's the death of the family I created, the dreams I had of growing old together, and the hope that my children would grow up with a better life than I had. But that grief is too messy for some friends, who don't want any of that negativity around them. My brothers are there for all of it. They see me at my worst and don't run. Instead, they support and remind me of what I look like when I'm at my best and that my pain is their pain.

"I remember all this as I look back at my brothers standing on the beach. I'm standing in the Pacific Ocean with the waters up to my neck. This sea isn't supposed to part like the Red one. Instead, this water will separate me now from some of the things I've been feeling leading up to this moment. This is my mikveh, my ritual bath to wash away the painful residue of divorce. I take one final breath before submerging myself. When I do, I can feel all the water moving around me. The waves push, and the undertow pulls. I think about everything we divided and what I packed to take to my new home. I think about how hard it was to tell the kids and admit my failures to my friends. I think about how plain the *get* [Jewish divorce agreement] looked next to our beautiful *ketubah* [Jewish wedding document]. Some of this begins to fade as the waters pass over. As I find my footing on the wet sand, I push my head up through the salty water. I feel the strife and anger leaving my body, washed away in the surf. I wipe the water from my eyes and see my brothers cheering for me and welcoming me home."

For Clergy: Adapting for Communal Settings
Clergy can offer a version of one of these blessings in front of the community:

> A marriage that has ended is like the first set of tablets and the covenant they represented. They were given in love, but then they were shattered. The Torah teaches that we carried them thereafter in the Ark of the Covenant along with the second set of tablets, which remained whole. As (the two of) you move into a new chapter of your lives, you carry with you hopes for new wholeness—and you also carry the broken pieces of your marriage, which are also holy, if shattered. At your wedding you vowed to betroth yourselves to each other in righteousness, in lovingkindness, and in compassion. May those same qualities be present as you disentangle your lives and separate from one another.[5]
> —*Rabbi Rachel Barenblat*

> God of the generations.
> As [name] sets out today with a new status,
> Let her/him/them journey with wholeness,
> Aware of her/his/their strength,
> Cognizant of her/his/their abilities to chart a new course
> Focused on gratitude for possibility and potential.
> Source of life, bless her/him/them with renewal.

Clergy invites the person marking divorce to respond publicly:

> God of Creation, this is a new beginning.
> May I recognize its light: *y'hi or*.

May I see its goodness: *ki tov*.
May I greet it with blessing.
May I mark it with holiness.

or

Give me strength as I walk a new path.
Open my eyes to the goodness before me.
Gird my footsteps with courage to move ahead each day.
Allow my hands to envelop those I love.
Encourage my soul to joy, my mind to trust.
Remind me to be patient with myself and others.
Open my heart to acknowledge peace.[6]

Words of Wisdom
The secret to a good divorce (or separation)
when there are children is to love your children
more than you hate your ex.

CHAPTER 11
Moving Forward After the Death of a Partner

It's a fearful thing to love
what death can touch.

A fearful thing to love,
hope, dream: to be—
to be, and oh! to lose.

A thing for fools this, and
a holy thing,
a holy thing to love.

For
your life has lived in me,
your laugh once lifted me,
your word was gift to me.

To remember this brings a painful joy.
'Tis a human thing, love,
a holy thing,
to love
what death has touched.[1]
—*Rabbi Chaim Stern*

Introduction

EVERYONE DIES either too early or too late; no one dies at the "right time." So whether the death of a loved one is expected or a shock, it is a moment that changes your life. Jewish tradition is very wise when it comes to rituals for mourning. These rituals include tearing a garment or a ribbon (*k'riah*, which reminds us that even in intense moments of grief we don't tear at ourselves but tear only a piece of cloth), sitting shivah for up to seven days, getting up from shivah to walk around the block with family or close friends to symbolize the mourner's moving forward, and reciting the memorial prayer (*Kaddish*) for the first month or year (reminding us that others have walked this path that we are now walking).[2]

All these practices are designed to support us in our grief and nestle us within a caring community. Yet even with these rituals, mourning isn't a linear path from one stage to another. Everyone mourns in their own way. But eventually, for most of us, the pain of the loss begins to be transformed into the blessing of memory.

This new ritual focuses on the moment that one might take off a wedding ring.

Questions to Consider

- What do you need at this moment to help you walk the path through this intense period of mourning?
- What might it take to help you to continue to move forward with compassion for yourself and for others who have experienced loss?

The Gathering

Time and Place

The moment you take off your wedding ring indicates you are now a widow/widower/solo ager. Perhaps for you that might be around the one-year anniversary of your partner's death or the wedding anniversary closest to the decision that it is time to take off the ring. A particularly resonant (but not the only) time, especially for Jews, might be a Saturday evening around *Havdalah*, the ceremony that marks the end of Shabbat. You can choose the time of the week that is most convenient for you. This ritual might take place at your home or the home of a close friend or family member or at the graveside.

People

Gather close friends and family, including those who were there for you during the most intense period of mourning or perhaps throughout the first year of mourning. You might ask one of them to serve as the ritual facilitator or invite a clergyperson. Let those invited know in advance that they will be invited to share some words about your marriage/partnership, as well as a wish or blessing for you.

Materials

Your ring
Your partner's ring
A small decorative bag or box to put them and keep them in
For Jews who choose to create a mezuzah, a *k'laf* (scroll for a mezuzah) that will be included with the rings in the decorative bag
Havdalah candle and something to light it with
Spices
Wine glass
Wine or grape juice
Glass for breaking (wrapped in cloth)

Ritual

Invite an intimate group to gather in community.

The ritual facilitator reads this poem:

> *The Cure*
> We think we get over things.
> We don't get over things.
> Or say, we get over measles
> but not a broken heart.
> We need to make that distinction.
> The things that become part of our experience
> never become less a part of our experience.
> How can I say it?
> The way to "get over" a life is to die.
> Short of that, you move with it,
> let the pain be pain,
> not in the hope that it will vanish
> but in the faith that it will fit in,
> find its place in the shape of things
> and be then not any less pain but true to form.
> Because anything natural has an inherent shape

and will flow towards it.
And a life is as natural as a leaf.
That's what we're looking for:
not the end of a thing but the shape of it.
Wisdom is seeing the shape of your life
without obliterating (getting over) a single
instant of it.³

—*Albert Huffstickler*

A friend/loved one says:

We wish for you the wisdom to see the shape of your life without getting over a single instant of it. And so we have gathered together for this transition.

The surviving partner says:

Through this year, with the help of all of you, I have learned that grieving is not about forgetting. As Rachel Naomi Remen wrote, "Grieving allows us to heal, to remember with love instead of with pain. It's a sorting process. One by one you let go of the things that are gone and mourn them. One by one you take hold of the things which have become a part of who you are and build again."⁴ My hope for this ceremony is that taking off my wedding ring in your supportive presence will make it possible for me to turn the pain of the loss of [name of departed partner] into the blessing of memory. This is the next step in my moving forward and building again. So first I want to say thank you. And second, I ask you to be witnesses to my moving forward and to continue to support me as I begin this next stage of my life.

A friend/loved one says:

Source of life and all Creation, who fashioned a covenant of love between [name of the deceased] and [name of the survivor]—a covenant of kindness and faithful trust, of justice and peace, of compassion and everlasting love. The wings of Your *Shechinah* helped them to guard and keep one another and now will keep [name of the deceased] in [name of the survivor]'s heart as you give them the courage, curiosity, sense of adventure, and strength to move forward. Bless this home as it becomes [the surviving partner]'s home, making room for a loving community. Blessed are You, Guardian of compassion, who renews the covenant.

The ritual facilitator or a friend holds up a *Havdalah* candle and says: This braided candle, glass of wine, and the spices represent the transition between the sweetness of Shabbat and the rest of the week. These symbols serve as a metaphor for the sweetness of memory as [the surviving partner] moves forward. We invite [the surviving partner] to say a few words of gratitude to all of you who have helped them through this difficult time and express what this transition means for them now.

The surviving partner speaks. Remarks might include thoughts about what this moment of transition means and some hopes going forward.

The ritual facilitator lights the candle and leads the group in the blessings:

בָּרוּךְ אַתָּה, יְיָ, אֱלֹהֵינוּ מֶלֶךְ הָעוֹלָם, בּוֹרֵא פְּרִי הַגָּפֶן.
Baruch atah, Adonai, Eloheinu Melech haolam, borei p'ri hagafen.
Blessed are You, Source of life and all Creation—
You create the fruit of the vine.

בָּרוּךְ אַתָּה, יְיָ, אֱלֹהֵינוּ מֶלֶךְ הָעוֹלָם, בּוֹרֵא מִינֵי בְשָׂמִים.
Baruch atah, Adonai, Eloheinu Melech haolam, borei minei v'samim.
Blessed are You, Source of life and all Creation—
You create the varied spices.

בָּרוּךְ אַתָּה, יְיָ, אֱלֹהֵינוּ מֶלֶךְ הָעוֹלָם, בּוֹרֵא מְאוֹרֵי הָאֵשׁ.
Baruch atah, Adonai, Eloheinu Melech haolam, borei m'orei ha-eish.
Blessed are You, Source of life and all Creation—
You create the fire's light.

Everyone present is invited to offer a blessing for the surviving partner by filling in this sentence with just one word:
As [the surviving partner] moves forward in their life, my blessing or wish for them is [one-word blessing].

Then the surviving partner extinguishes the *Havdalah* candle by dunking it in the wine and says:

> Weddings end with the breaking of a glass. At our wedding, [the deceased's name] and I did this together. Now I break a glass alone, symbolizing—as the first broken glass did—that the world we live in is broken. In our marriage, both of us had worked in our own ways to repair the broken world. In breaking the glass alone, I commit to continue to do that work as I go forward in this next stage of my life.

The surviving partner places the rings in the bag, adds a *k'laf* (parchment) if the intention is to have the bag serve as a mezuzah, and hangs the bag in an appropriate spot in the house, which will continue to welcome a loving community of family and friends, old and new, young and old.

Laura's Story

"After the unveiling for my husband, Richard, thirteen months after his death at age seventy, I knew I wanted to take off my wedding ring. Many women never take off their rings, moving them to the other hand or making them into necklaces. Others take them off without ceremony, when suddenly it feels right. For me, taking off the wedding ring was a statement that I was now a solo ager. My wedding ring had signaled to the world that I was in a relationship with a partner, which was no longer true. While the word 'widow' was a painful description of this stage, I needed to admit that it was in fact my truth. I was no longer a married woman, I needed a ritual to acknowledge that divinity was present, even in the truth of this loss."

For Clergy: Adapting for Communal Settings

For people who are connected to a synagogue community, the rabbi could offer a blessing during the Torah service, or—if this is on the first *yahrzeit*—the surviving partner could speak about their beloved and take off the ring. Alternatively, this could be part of a communal *Havdalah* service.

For clergy of other faiths, blessings could be incorporated into a service at the birthday of the deceased, the anniversary of the death, or on the date closest to the taking off of the ring.

Words of Wisdom

In Blackwater Woods

To live in this world

you must be able
to do three things:
to love what is mortal;
to hold it

against your bones knowing
your own life depends on it;
and, when the time comes to let it go,
to let it go.[5]

—Mary Oliver

CHAPTER 12

Beginning a New Relationship

It is not good for a person to be alone.
—*Genesis 2:18*

Introduction

HUMAN BEINGS crave intimacy, both emotional and physical, at every age. It was true when we were younger, and it is still true now for most of us. Some of us have been partnered, others not. For those who once were, the death of a spouse or the end of a committed relationship through separation or divorce has left us as solo agers. And now, through serendipity or intention, we find ourselves beginning a new relationship. It comes with the hope that the loneliness we might have felt will end and that we'll now have someone with whom to share adventure, fun, and intimacy. It also comes with the wisdom about relationships that we have learned through our life experience. This moment is one of gratitude for the opportunity to begin something new and at the same time—especially in the case of a person whose beloved spouse has died—a moment of loss or even guilt. For some, it is best marked as a private moment between the two partners; for others, it is a public moment to be acknowledged and celebrated in the presence of close family or friends.

It is important to make clear that even if the ceremony is public, it is not a wedding. Whether private or public, it still can be a sacred moment.

Questions to Consider

- How is choosing to move in together different from choosing to continue to live separately? What are the differences that matter most?
- What are you signaling to other people if your ceremony is public?

- Will this ceremony have an impact on your adult children (if you have them)?
- What kind of a commitment are you making to each other?
- What are the financial dimensions of this new relationship?

The Gathering

(For a private ceremony between the two of you if you are not moving in together.)

Time and Place

Do this when it is clear to each of you and to others that you have become a couple. The place to do this is at the doorpost of your bedroom in each of your homes.

People

This ritual is for just you two or a few close friends and family.

Materials

A mezuzah
Seed paper
A pot (or outdoor garden) or planting

Ritual

Each person takes a piece of seed paper and writes an intention or a hope for this relationship.

Read the intentions to one another.

Plant the seed paper in a pot or a garden.

Enter one of the homes and affix a mezuzah on the doorpost of the bedroom. Say this blessing:

בָּרוּךְ אַתָּה, יְיָ, אֱלֹהֵינוּ מֶלֶךְ הָעוֹלָם,
אֲשֶׁר קִדְּשָׁנוּ בְּמִצְוֹתָיו, וְצִוָּנוּ לִקְבֹּעַ מְזוּזָה.

*Baruch atah, Adonai, Eloheinu Melech haolam,
asher kid'shanu b'mitzvotav v'tzivanu likboa m'zuzah.*

Blessed are You, Source of life and all Creation, who makes us holy through connections and connects us to each other and to You through affixing the mezuzah.

Recite the *Sh'ma*:

שְׁמַע יִשְׂרָאֵל יְיָ אֱלֹהֵינוּ יְיָ אֶחָד.

Sh'ma, Yisrael! Adonai Eloheinu, Adonai echad.

Hear, O Israel! The Eternal is our God, the Eternal alone.

Invoke the angel blessing:

בְּשֵׁם יְיָ אֱלֹהֵי יִשְׂרָאֵל
מִימִינִי מִיכָאֵל וּמִשְּׂמֹאלִי גַבְרִיאֵל
וּמִלְּפָנַי אוּרִיאֵל וּמֵאֲחוֹרַי רְפָאֵל
וְעַל רֹאשִׁי שְׁכִינַת אֵל.

B'shem Adonai, Elohei Yisrael
Mimini Michael umismoli Gavriel
Umilfanai Uriel umei-achorai R'fael
V'al roshi Shechinat El.

In the name of *Adonai*, the God of Israel:
May the angel Michael be at my right,
and the angel Gabriel be at my left,
and in front of me the angel Uriel,
and behind me the angel Raphael,
and above my head the *Shechinah* [Divine Presence].

Conclude with the *Shehecheyanu*:

בָּרוּךְ אַתָּה, יְיָ, אֱלֹהֵינוּ מֶלֶךְ הָעוֹלָם,
שֶׁהֶחֱיָנוּ וְקִיְּמָנוּ וְהִגִּיעָנוּ לַזְּמַן הַזֶּה.

Baruch atah, Adonai, Eloheinu Melech haolam,
shehecheyanu v'kiy'manu v'higianu laz'man hazeh.

Blessed are You, Source of life and all Creation—
You have kept us in life, sustained us, and brought us
to this moment of a new beginning.

Soon after, do the same ceremony at the other partner's home.

> **Beginning a New Relationship in a
> Continuing Care Retirement Community**
>
> Sometimes new relationships begin in senior living communities such as continuing care retirement communities (CCRC), facilitated by social and cultural events organized within the community. Intimate connections, whether sexual or platonic, can diminish loneliness and increase joy. Yet these new relationships might be challenging to the families of residents or create awkward situations for staff who might not be aware of these relationships. A ritual or ceremony that acknowledges a special bond between two residents who choose to spend time together, eat together, and often want privacy in their rooms can normalize and celebrate these connections, even with the knowledge that these relationships might not continue over the time the residents are in the CCRC. A simple ritual with family (if appropriate), other residents, and staff could acknowledge gratitude for having found a companion for this moment of their lives. The partners could say to each other, "We are grateful to have found a companion like the one mentioned in Jewish tradition: 'Get a companion to eat with, drink with, study with, sleep with, and reveal secrets to, the secrets of the Torah and the secrets of worldly things'" (*Avot D'Rabbi Natan* 8:3). A family member or friend might offer an informal blessing. The ceremony could conclude with everyone present singing the *Shehecheyanu*.

Michael and Caryl's Story

Michael and Caryl found each other again after almost sixty years. They were college sweethearts, but they went on to marry other people, raise families, and build careers. After those earlier marriages had ended, Michael decided to search for Caryl on the internet. Always a gifted researcher, he found her contact information and called. Michael identified himself and asked, "Do you remember me?" Caryl's response was, "Are you kidding?"

They still seemed to have much in common. Both retired from careers as educators in science. Curious to see what Michael looked like after all these years, Caryl agreed to meet him. She knew she would recognize him right away. But just to be sure he recognized her, she carried a copy of *Alice in Wonderland* with her (a book with special significance for them both). They walked for miles and talked for hours. When he returned home, he sent her a recording of Gustav Mahler's *Des Knaben Wunderhorn*.

After a long-distance romance that lasted several months, they decided to move in together. Michael moved to New York. Both in their late seventies, they then chose to get married. They had a Jewish ceremony in California, arranged by Caryl's daughter, with their grandchildren holding the four poles of the chuppah, the wedding canopy. At the celebration party that followed, everyone danced to klezmer music. Past and present photos of the wedding couple were on display.

When each was asked what the most positive qualities are of relationships at this age, they both said that the companionship is wonderful, especially with somebody you really care about and who cares about you. Michael said that he learned a lot from Caryl's example of the values of loyalty, caring, unreserved affection, and strong family connections. And what did Caryl learn from him? "This relationship taught me that there are many different kinds of love. Each one has a special place in your heart." The advice they have for others contemplating a many-decades-later second time around is, "Don't expect it to be like the first relationship. It's different. You are not growing old together; you are already there."

Jeff and Donna's Story

"As single people in our fifties who were looking for a partner to love and spend the rest of our lives together, we both hoped that family and friends would introduce us to potential life partners. When that didn't happen, we both reluctantly jumped on Match.com. What first had me intrigued was Jeff's statement that he was 'looking for my last first date.' For Jeff, it was my positive attitude and energy. Little did we know that a glance at both of our profiles would change both of our lives forever. Our first conversation off of Match.com was September 7, 2010. Our first date was September 11, 2010. We were engaged on November 10, 2011, and married September 23, 2012."

For Clergy: Adapting for Communal Settings

A clergyperson or other community member might say:

Today we celebrate the loving commitment of [name of partner one] and [name of partner two] to each other, and we share in their joy. In Song of Songs 6:3, we read, "*Ani l'dodi v'dodi li*—I am my beloved's, and my beloved is mine." This represents not only God's relationship with Israel, but also the commitment that is shared between [name of partner one] and [name of partner two]. Love lives as long as the human heart beats, as long as we draw breath. The soul reaches out to another, recognizing a kindred spirit. Today we acknowledge [name of partner one] and [name of partner two]'s loving commitment to one another. May they find sustenance in their relationship and enjoyment in each other. May their physical presence strengthen their spiritual growth. May they nurture their fragility and rely on their strength. May their days be full, and enriched with love. Amen.[1]

Words of Wisdom

Love knows no age.
—*Folk saying*

PART THREE

*Bodies Changing,
Caregiving, and Caregetting*

CHAPTER 13
Needing Something to Lean On

My body is a story I tell and retell myself, variations
in a grateful or grieving key.[1]
—Nessa Rapoport

Introduction

GROWING OLDER is often challenging. Our bodies are changing and becoming more fragile. More of our friends report stories of falling and the sometimes difficult descriptions of hospital visits or physical therapy. The wise ones among us add bars to our showers and banisters to our stairs. Eventually some of us will need help walking, perhaps with a cane, a walker, a wheelchair. Many of us see this transition to a mobility device as a loss or even a source of shame. That might lead to waiting too long to have something to lean on or to ask for help when we need it. The same is true about using a hearing aid. While hearing aid technology has improved over the years, some older adults don't want to admit they have difficulty hearing in some settings and as a result are not fully able to participate in conversations or public events. According to Paul Irving, writing in the *Wall Street Journal*, "Even among hearing-aid users, most lived with hearing loss for more than 10 years before seeking help."[2]

When this time comes, a ritual or even a simple blessing—ideally in the presence of family and close friends—can help transform this moment of transition from shame and loss to gratitude that we can continue to live with energy and joy thanks to the support of our community and the help that comes with new technology.

Questions to Consider

- What can you do before this moment arrives to help you prepare for it?

- What would it mean to you to expand your definition of health and to call having manageable issues as "healthy with conditions"? For example, some people are healthy with diabetes that is managed with insulin, or healthy with cancer that is managed by radiation, or healthy with heart disease that is managed with medicine and exercise, or healthy with hearing loss or vision loss that is managed with hearing aids or eyeglasses, or healthy with mobility issues that are managed with mobility aids and physical therapy.
- What words of gratitude might you say to your body at this moment?

The Gathering

Time and Place

Hold this ritual when you are ready, at your home (ideally a place with a garden).

People

Invite close friends and family.

Materials

Incense like those used in the purification of the ancient Temple (frankincense or myrrh)

Assistive device (e.g., for mobility, hearing, vision), depending on the specific circumstance of the transition

Ritual

Friends and family gather. The guest of honor begins by thanking those assembled and shares what this transition means for them, emphasizing their gratitude that they are lucky enough to continue to be actively engaged in the world in spite of this transition. They might also share some reflections on all the places and experiences their body has enabled them to have enjoyed over the years.

The guest of honor then offers a prayer:

Eternal One, Source of life, help me to find the strength to acknowledge that my soul and my body are miraculous gifts.

Allow me to accept, with willingness and gratitude, the [number] years You have already given me to inhabit my body. Open my heart to balance what is difficult for me with the openness to discover new ways of moving/seeing/hearing, so that I may feel the support of this community surrounding me and help others do the same. Eternal One, Source of life, You provide me with all my needs.

If the focus is on mobility loss, the subject might say:

Eternal One, Source of life, help me to acknowledge that although I cannot walk without help, I can still move forward. Open my senses so that I may hear, smell, see, touch, and taste the world around me in new ways. Help me to realize the value of being still. Allow me to mourn the loss of my independence, and allow me the courage to know that I do not need to walk without help (or to walk with my feet) to walk in Your ways. As Psalm 37:23–24 teaches, "A person's steps are made firm by the Divine . . . though one stumbles, they do not fall down because they are supported by the Divine Presence."[3] Blessed are You, Source of life and all Creation—You make firm each person's steps.

If the focus is on hearing loss that has begun as one gets older, the subject might say:

As I acknowledge that my hearing acuity is diminishing, I want to remember the story in the Bible about Elijah the prophet and his encounter with the Divine. He hears the Divine call out, "Go out and stand on the mountain before the Eternal." And then, "the Eternal passed by, and a great and strong wind tore the mountains and broke in pieces the rocks . . . but the Eternal was not in the wind. And after the wind, an earthquake, but the Eternal was not in the earthquake. And after the earthquake, a fire, but the Eternal was not in the fire. And after the fire, the sound of a low whisper, a still small voice" (I Kings 19:11–12). Though I cannot hear as well as I used to, I can clearly hear that still small voice calling me to be open-hearted, compassionate, honest, and present with the people I love. May I remember beautiful sounds that I have heard throughout my life—music, poetry, bird song, laughter—and be grateful for sounds I continue to hear. May I have the courage to acknowledge when I cannot follow a conversation, to ask people to repeat or rephrase what they have said, and to face me when they speak. May I continue to explore new technologies designed to assist hearing, and may I continue, without embarrassment, to be engaged in conversation and culture. May I remember that the central instruction of Jewish tradition is to listen, *Sh'ma Yisrael*, and through listening in whatever way I can, I will be reminded that everything is connected and I am part of a larger whole.

שְׁמַע יִשְׂרָאֵל יְיָ אֱלֹהֵינוּ יְיָ אֶחָד.

Sh'ma, Yisrael! Adonai Eloheinu, Adonai echad.

Hear, O Israel! The Eternal is our God, the Eternal alone.

If the focus is on vision loss, the person might say:

Though my world may be darker now than it was before, help me to see that it is also filled with great light and beauty. Source of life, help me to see what I might have never seen before—or known to look for. Help me to see the world with my hands, with my ears, with my nose, with my tongue, with my heart. Open my heart to the wisdom of Torah and the beauty of kindness and compassion. Allow me to be human in my vulnerability and to radiate light even as I can no longer see it with my eyes.

וְהָאֵר עֵינֵינוּ בְּתוֹרָתֶךָ.

V'ha-eir eineinu b'Toratecha.

Open our eyes to Your Torah.

Participants each light the incense they have brought, and then say together:

May the sweet smell of this incense release any negative energy and bring gratitude, joy, and delight into [name]'s life as they move forward.[4]

—*Tamara Arnow, adapted*

Conclude with this version of the *Shehecheyanu* (written by Ilana Schatz):

בָּרוּךְ אַתָּה, יְיָ, אֱלֹהֵינוּ, מֶלֶךְ הָעוֹלָם, שֶׁהֶחֱיָנִי, וְקִיְּמָנִי, וּתְמָכְנִי.

*Baruch atah, Adonai, Eloheinu Melech haolam,
shehecheyani, v'kiy'mani, ut'machani.*

Blessed are You, Source of life and all Creation, who has brought me to this moment, sustained me, and provided me with support.

Next, participants can offer one-word blessings:

As [name] makes this transition, I wish for them [one-word blessing].

Conclude with some music that feels right for you.

Marion's Story

"Every morning of every day for the past fifty years, I've walked across Twenty-Third Street and back to work, shop, and check in with all my friends in my Manhattan neighborhood. Stopping by the newspaper seller, the grocer, the shoemaker, and my neighbors sitting on park benches (only in the nice weather, of course) gives me great satisfaction. I know every person's name and what ails them, and I help my friends out whenever I can. These days, I am less steady on my feet. Luckily, I have my beautiful flamingo-pink cane, which helps me to go the distance. My cousin in California sent it to me. She knows it's one of my favorite colors, and I like to coordinate it with my spring and summer outfits. I take my cane everywhere; it's become my signature accessory."

Paul's Story

"For my wife, Susie, it started with our TV at high volume. Then it was her retreat from conversations in noisy restaurants and conversations at work. We'd joke that it wasn't her hearing, it was that after so many years together she'd heard all she wanted from me. Energetic and smart, Susie was reticent to deal with her hearing loss, fearing that hearing aids would make her look weak or feeble. A successful real-estate agent in Los Angeles, she knew that younger people are presumed to be more effective and that ageist attitudes are deeply rooted in business, social institutions, and the broader culture. She had overheard slights about older agents in town. Her concerns that hearing aids might signify decline and diminished capacity had to be balanced against the prospect of better hearing. Eventually, after many conversations with friends, she took the leap. . . . Maybe if we had a ceremony of some sort it might have been easier for her."[5]

Ilana's Story

"On a wildflower hike last year, someone approaching us on the trail exclaimed, 'What a beautiful chariot you have!' (referring to my manual wheelchair). I loved that re-frame, and given that I'll be spending up to sixteen or seventeen hours a day in my power wheelchair, I've chosen to think of it as my *merkavah* [chariot]—referring to Ezekiel's vision. I hope to be held by the Divine Spirit as I travel with it."

Roger's Story

"My mother moved to a senior living community when she was in her mid-eighties. She brought her car with her. It was obvious to me and my siblings that she shouldn't be driving—obvious to everyone except her. My siblings and I agreed to try to convince her to give up the keys, but she resisted. She was still a good driver, she protested, even after she had backed out of her niece's driveway on to a low wall. And how would she explain to her friends that her kids had taken away her keys? How could she still be independent and get to the places she still wanted to go? My siblings and I shared with her research we had done about ride-sharing options and showed her how to use gogograndparents.com, which makes it easy for a person without a smartphone to call an Uber or Lyft. I took her for a ride in a driverless car—she was scared but actually curious. And then her granddaughter made an impassioned plea that she give her the car for her cross-country trip to a new job. Mom relented, now able to explain to her friends that she was giving up the car because she was generous. My siblings and I, relieved and grateful, told her we knew she was wise and took her out to dinner to celebrate. It was a kind of ritual."

For Clergy: Adapting for Communal Settings
Clergy can convene a group of community members who have recently begun to rely on mobility devices. The informal group, perhaps led by a social worker, encourages participants to share their feelings about their mobility loss and strategies for making the transition positive. We suggest the group discuss the chapter titled "I Am My Body; I Am Not My Body" in *Wise Aging: Living with Joy, Resilience and Spirit* by Rabbi Rachel Cowan and Dr. Linda Thal, and the chapter titled "Regarding My Body" by Nessa Rapoport in *Getting Good at Getting Older.* After a period of study and sharing, the group could be invited to make a presentation to the larger community as models for how to talk about complicated transitions. The presentation might also include strategies for the communal institution to make it easier for people with limited mobility to fully participate in programs and activities of the community.

Clergy could invite all the members of the community who had given up driving in the past year and give them a special blessing for the wisdom they demonstrated by knowing that that time had come. The power of this public acknowledgment is that now the synagogue or church has a stake in helping them continue to get around without a car—so they could continue to come to services and events or get to a medical appointment. This could lead to a new effort on the part of the community to set up a rideshare project, enlisting members to volunteer to be drivers. Imagine high school students or young adults who grew up in the congregation being part of this effort and the connections that could blossom between elders and youngers in the congregation.

Words of Wisdom

Let's look at our lives as squarely, and as lovingly, as we can. And let's not be deflected by concerns about our bodies, their images and their illnesses, from what is most significant about our selves: that we can grow in courage, in grit, in spirit, not in spite of who we are but because of who we are.[6]

—*Nancy Mairs*

CHAPTER 14

Coming Out with Memory Loss

Waking from his sleep, Jacob said,
"Truly, the Eternal is in this place, and I did not know it!"
—*Genesis 28:16*

Introduction

THERE ARE a lot of jokes about memory loss. Two older people are sitting on a bench. One says to the other, "We will always be old friends until we are senile. Then we can be new friends." Or: "I told my doctor I was having problems with my memory. He made me pay in advance." While memory issues often come along with aging and are quite normal, some memory issues are not at all funny. As we grow older, some of us will develop dementia or some other condition that leads to memory loss. You probably know someone with Alzheimer's disease or someone caring for a loved one with it.

Indeed, nearly seven million Americans are living with Alzheimer's. By 2050, this number is projected to rise to nearly thirteen million. Over eleven million Americans provide unpaid care for people with Alzheimer's or other dementias. Seventy percent of dementia caregivers say that coordinating care is stressful. Two-thirds also have difficulty finding resources and support for their own needs. Seventy-four percent of dementia caregivers say that they are concerned about maintaining their own health since becoming a caregiver. About one in nine people age sixty-five and older (10.9 percent) has Alzheimer's. About 30 percent of caregivers are age sixty-five or older.[1]

Until recently, many people diagnosed with Alzheimer's tried to keep it a secret, fearing they would be excluded from social events or over time become isolated from friends. Sometimes the one with memory loss wants to acknowledge it, but others close to them are in denial, wanting yet another test or doctor to say it isn't true. Now, however, more and more, people are "coming out" by acknowledging what is happening. And others of us are "coming out" as caregivers for someone we love. When both the one with Alzheimer's and the primary caregivers are open about the diagnosis, it becomes easier to ask for support and to develop strategies for making the transition to this new reality easier for everyone. It might also make it easier to develop a different language for speaking about Alzheimer's and help us see that those with dementia can still be respected for who they were, who they are, and who they can still be. An intimate ritual or a simple blessing in the presence of friends and or family can create an openness that could enable this to make this next stage a bit easier.

> Approximately two-thirds of caregivers are women; more specifically, over one-third of dementia caregivers are daughters. Most caregivers (66 percent) live with the person with dementia. Approximately one-quarter of dementia caregivers are "sandwich generation" caregivers, meaning that they care not only for an aging parent but also for at least one child.[2]

Questions to Consider
- What can we learn from people we know who have navigated this path before us?
- What are the resources our community offers to help us?
- What might be some of the financial implications of this new diagnosis?
- When might a decision be made about bringing in outside caregiving?
- At what point might we need to decide to move the one with Alzheimer's to a care facility?

The Gathering
Time and Place

This ritual is designed to be held at home, when the caregiver and the one with dementia recognize the diagnosis.

People

Gather close family and friends.

Materials

Small rocks
A basket or bag to hold the rocks
Art markers for writing on the rocks

Ritual

Gather close family and friends in a circle of support.

Begin with a poem read by a participant:

Prayer for People with Dementia and Their Caregivers
Dementia comes
like a thief in the night,
then stays,
a dark shadow,
ever-present,
entwining itself within the brain.

Healing Presence,
do not abandon [name of person]
in their time of need
and great distress,
in this time of transition.
Enfold them and their family
and all those who care for them
under the wings of Shekinah,
Bless them with peace, tranquility, calm
in the midst of the whirlwind
of this terrible illness.

Healing Presence,
grant strength, patience, and wisdom
to all those who care for them
and for all those who suffer with dementia.

Healing Presence,
grant strength, wisdom, and perseverance
to the scientists who work tirelessly
to untangle the web of this disease,

to catch this thief that comes in the night
and takes the mind and spirit.

Healing Presence,
while there is no cure,
grant us hope
and healing—
hope and healing for acceptance
of what cannot be changed,
hope and healing for strength
for what lies ahead,
hope and healing
for wholeness, shalom.³
—*Ariel Neshama Lee*

Next, choose one of the following prayers to be offered by the one with Alzheimer's:

God of compassion, in this moment of fear and dread, I turn to You. Lead me through the wilderness; speak to me with tenderness—for You are my hope.

Here, in a foreign land of illness, I long for the familiar: the gentle comfort of loved ones, places I know, things I enjoy. May these sustain me and keep me connected to the world. Bless my days with tiny joys.

And let there be unhurried time with family and friends. I pray that, when I am weak, their arms will embrace me. I pray that in my silences they will understand me. In valleys of darkness, may their voices guide me and reassure me. I give thanks for the gift of their patience and love.

May solace come in the sweetness of song, in the beauty of nature, and feelings too deep for words. God, be with me when I feel alone. Accompany my loved ones as they walk in the shadow of my illness.

When confusion takes hold, soothe my spirit, calm my fears. My God of compassion, answer me. And even when I cannot ask, answer me. Heal and comfort those who are ill. Lead us through the wilderness—for You are our hope.[4]

Or:

My God, I am about to enter a wilderness.
All that I have thought is me—
my voice, my thinking, my memories—
will slip away, and I may not even comprehend it.

As I enter this wilderness, my step quivers and my soul hurts.
In this leap of faith, I will come to rely on so many and we will all rely on You.

Whom will I recognize? Who will recognize me?
Even though my mind will change, please do not let the knitting of my soul unravel.
Only You will know me, even if I do not know myself.

Please help me to remember that others before me have found You in the wilderness.
I am not sure I will know to look for You.
But please, look for me.[5]

A participant might say:

This wilderness is bewildering in so many ways, yet God is in this place too. Like Jacob, we gather rocks—symbolic pillows—with words of blessing and encouragement. Please take a moment to write a one-word blessing for our friend/family member. Examples include resilience, patience, compassion, gentleness, gratitude.

After participants write their one-word blessing on the rocks, each participant reads their word. Then the blessings are gathered in a basket and given to the person at the center of the ritual.

Conclude with a song of your choice or the last verse of the poem with which we began:

Healing Presence,
while there is no cure,

grant us hope
and healing—
hope and healing for acceptance
of what cannot be changed,
hope and healing for strength
for what lies ahead,
hope and healing
for wholeness, shalom.

> **A Caregiver's Piggy Bank**
>
> As my mother cared lovingly for my father through his early onset of Alzheimer's until his death, I asked how she managed. She responded, "If I had put a penny in a piggy bank for every loving thing Dad did for me over the years, the bank would be so full that even if I took a penny out for each day of his illness, I would never empty the bank."[6]
>
> Time changes when the brain fails, becoming strange and plastic.... Dementia gives us an opportunity to question how time and language and perception work. It strikes me that both artistic and religious practice have these qualities: new ways to use words, repetition, pauses and silences, gestures and images—expressions of the expansive interior longing to be heard... an opportunity to question how time and language and perception work.[7]
>
> For some people, dementia may lead to a time when the ill person no longer recognizes people they love, including their partners. When that time has come, it might lead to a decision on the part of the healthy partner to move forward in their lives and seek companionship and intimacy with another person while they remain committed to the loving care and financial support of the demented partner, with the assurance that this decision will not bring shame or embarrassment to them. Sometimes it is helpful to affirm in the presence of a community of friends and family that the healthy partner should feel free to live as full a life as possible and a new partner can be welcomed into the community of friends.[8]

Marge's Story

"I got to know Radelle about five years ago through Chai Village LA, a partnership between two synagogues where members age in place and develop close social and caring connections. Three years ago, as we drove to a Chai Village retreat, I began to notice Radelle's symptoms. Radelle drove and her sense of direction wasn't what it was, and she was always misplacing her keys, which really frustrated her. Upon our return to Los Angeles, encouraged by another rider in the car, I made the difficult decision to call her daughter. Turns out that I was the second concerned friend who had called. Shortly thereafter, her daughter took her to the neurologist for a diagnostic test, which turned out to be positive for Alzheimer's. Although she doesn't remember the moment of the diagnosis, I know that at that point she decided she was going to tell people in her circle what was happening with her. There was no ritual, but when she would grope for the right word in a conversation with old or new friends she would say, 'Pardon me, but I have Alzheimer's and I need help with the correct word!'

"I find her positive energy inspiring. She is never a victim. She decided to move from her lovely two-bedroom condo in her gated community, where she was an integral part of the activities there, and scale down her belongings to fit into a one-bedroom suite in an assisted-living senior community not too far away. She loves her new lifestyle there without looking back on what was, only enjoying what is now! She still attends family gatherings, both locally and out of town. She cherishes the times with her daughter. Two loving granddaughters visit her on a weekly basis, and they get manicures and pedicures and go shopping together, making a wonderful ritual of memories for her friends and family. Her old friends from work and temple still take her out and about, and Radelle embraces her new friends at the assisted-living senior community and has made activities there an integral part of her life. Each time I see her, a little slice of who she once was is missing, but she loves all who she is today and has become an incredible role model to her friends and family! I am also struck by the power of a community of friends to keep her connected to the world. She doesn't have one caregiver, though someday she might, but she does have a circle of friends who share the caregiving—the transportation, the visits, the activities, the participation in temple and village programs, and the willingness to be patient and loving, celebrating who she is instead of mourning what she has lost.

"Would a ritual have been helpful to share her new life with her friends and family, getting all her friends together to share her news? Perhaps; however, Radelle chose to do it her way, on a one-on-one basis."

Debra's Story

"My first true inkling of Peter's dementia was at a restaurant when he said he could not calculate tips. I remember exactly where I was sitting. It was the first of hundreds of small shocks that burned themselves into my memory. There is a drawer in my brain with ten years' worth of snapshots or sound bites of such moments: a phone call that he is lost in the rain on a street corner in Manhattan, a wastebasket thrown down the garbage chute with the trash, a critical document fed into the shredder instead of the copier. That night at the restaurant, we saw none of that coming, but I must have sensed the possibility.... I had no idea what it meant to be the wife of a husband with Alzheimer's disease when our doctor in New Jersey first wrote 'possible dementia' in Peter's chart in the fall of 2014. It took my breath away, but I thought, 'I can handle this.' Some preparation was easy. I found support groups for us both. I did my research and shared it with him. Knowing the years were limited, I began planning trips from our bucket list. I arranged updated legal documents.

"It was the little things that began to overwhelm me. I was constantly 'on'—on the lookout for signs of his decline so I could create a work-around. It was like whack-a-mole. Adjust, adjust, adjust. Manage, manage, manage. The fixes could be simple but the quantity—and the time they consumed—increased over the months, then years. His losses were my gains in the worst possible way. Every chore he could not handle moved to my to-do list.

"I was strapped into a front-row seat for his decline. Each time his life shifted, mine did too. He was losing pieces of himself, and I was losing him. There is a name for this experience: ambiguous loss. 'Ambiguous loss is a type of loss you feel when a person with dementia is physically here, but may not be mentally or emotionally present in the same way as before.'[9] In dementia's cruel twist, the less Peter was 'with' me emotionally, the more he was physically present in my life. We moved through the world even more as a couple, but I was feeling more and more alone.

"In 2016 I started a list on my computer of Peter's inabilities. They were coming fast and furious. One day as I skimmed the list preparing to record another incident, a switch flipped. What was I doing? Alzheimer's disease was relentless. The list of what he could no longer do would inevitably grow longer. In a flash I saw that recording his losses was objectifying him. It was a way to hold him and his illness at arm's length, to hold back the grief growing inside me. Was this what I wanted to do for the years we had left? Would this lessen the pain when he became incapacitated and inevitably died?

"With one click I created a new list. This one enumerated his wonderful qualities, the things that made him happiest, and how he contributed to our family and the world. Peter ushered at the temple. Peter laughed at puns. Peter loved a good glass of scotch with friends. Peter kayaked and hiked and told great stories. I started looking to create more moments like that for us both. I tried to take pleasure in the simple things we shared and be grateful while they remained. I didn't want to lose the Peter I loved—a multifaceted person who did not deserve to be defined by his deficits.

"Peter and I resonated deeply with the teaching that each person is created *b'tzelem Elohim*, 'in God's image'—capable of goodness, kindness, and justice. As I now paid closer attention to the beautiful image of God in Peter, I was in awe of the grace with which he lived with his dementia. He never hid his disease or was ashamed to ask for help. His passion for explaining his dementia to others was for him an act of *tikkun olam* [fixing the world]—a way to make life easier perhaps for someone else. It gave him purpose.

"On Peter's sixty-sixth birthday, we met with his neurologist. I needed her professional advice about the expected speed of his decline. Could I work another year? I wanted to be living near our middle daughter in California for support when Peter reached the last stages of this disease. When would be a good time to move? She replied, 'Tomorrow.' She urged us to do this while Peter could still adjust to a new place and new people. So in the fall I drove us cross-country to our new home. In many ways we had a lovely first year. We welcomed our first grandchildren. I found a support group. Peter made some new friends.

"One day, a man in my support group reminded me, 'Anyone can be a caregiver, but only you can be his wife.' I knew it was time to do what Peter and I had agreed upon years earlier. He moved to a memory care unit and called it his second home. Now a team did the caregiving, and I did the fun things. I took him out for meals, walks, and visits with friends.

"The last two quieter years have given me time to practice moving through the world on my own, in preparation for when Peter is truly gone. I choose activities and friends carefully, saying no to situations that I now know might trigger stress. I am still recovering. I live every day with anticipatory grief by my side and am not sure what I will feel when he dies. I do know that others will be there to embrace me when that time comes.

"Most days I sit by his bed talking to Peter for an hour or so. Music he used to enjoy plays in the background. He often stares at the ceiling or falls back asleep. I might feed him his lunch or dinner. On Fridays, I sing his favorite Shabbat songs. I hold his hand during the healing prayer. Sometimes he looks me in the eye, and I wonder what he sees.

"I know what I see. I see the gentle man who trusted me with his dignity, safety, and happiness. I see the husband who let me love him through it all and never stopped loving me in return. I see the soul behind his beautiful eyes, where his spark is waiting to be released. I want to hold onto it, but I know soon I will have to let it go. I hope I will be ready."[10]

For Clergy: Adapting for Communal Settings
This is a moment that some may not want to mark in a communal way. For those who do, considering the preferences of the people involved, such as moving to a clergy office or an intimate sanctuary for this ritual.

Words of Wisdom

Changing my words and conversations changed my attitude from watching myself lose things to embracing what I still had.[11]

—*Myrna Marofsky*

CHAPTER 15

Becoming a Caregiver or Caregetter

There are four kinds of people in the world: those who have been caregivers; those who are currently caregivers; those who will be caregivers; and those who will need caregivers.[1]
—*Rosalynn Carter*

Introduction

WE KNOW that the words of the former first lady are accurate. Many of us have already been caregivers—to young children, to aging parents, to beloved friends, to intimate partners. Many of us still are caregivers. And we know that many of us will—or will again—be caregivers. We are learning that one of the many challenges that come along with this role is that it sometimes unfolds slowly, invisible to those around us. In some cases, it begins by making sure that our loved ones are safe at home, with support bars, walk-in tubs, or security devices. Over time, more of our time is spent accompanying those we love to appointments with health providers or sitting with them as they receive dialysis or some other kind of medical treatment. Sometimes, as is often the case with a hip or knee replacement, those we care for return to health and no longer need that kind of support; sometimes, however, more help is needed. Sometimes the role of caregiver falls to one person unexpectedly, when distance or circumstances make it harder for others to participate in caregiving. This can lead to resentment on the part of the primary caregiver and guilt or judgment on the part of others who feel responsibility—all feelings that are hard to discuss.

Additionally, there may come a time in our lives when we become caregetters, the ones needing care. This too is hard. For some people, admitting that they need help feels like a failure or a challenge to their self-image. After all, Americans place a high priority on being self-reliant, which makes offering help to others much easier than accepting help ourselves. Denial is a powerful and dangerous strategy that often leads to a person risking their safety and health by declining to admit what is happening and accepting that they need care. These feelings are also hard to talk about.

There is not one definable moment when one becomes a caregiver. For some, it might be when a loved one can no longer perform basic self-care tasks like dressing, bathing, or transferring from one body position to another. For another, it might be the moment when a caregiver joins a support group to have a safe place to talk about the stress of this new role. For still another, it might be the moment when a primary caregiver decides to gather adult children or close friends who can help with the tasks of caregiving. So too, there is not one moment when a person becomes a caregetter. For some, it might be hospitalization or coming home after being hospitalized and not being able to take care of themselves without help. For others, there might be a general sense that now is the time to acknowledge caregetting needs. This lack of clarity also makes this a difficult topic to discuss.

A useful meditation phrase for this moment might be: It's like this now. It's like this now, different from what it used to be like. It's like this now, and we don't know what it will be like in the future. What we have is now. This moment. This transition.

Not everyone will want to ritualize these transitions, because they represent a loss that is unwelcome. But for those open to ritual, ceremony, or blessing, doing something in the presence of close family or friends may make this difficult transition a little bit easier. It also provides an opportunity to talk about all of these complicated feelings.

The template we offer can be adapted to a ritual or ceremony for becoming a caregiver, becoming a caregetter, or both. It can be private or public. Feel free to adapt, rewrite, or reimagine what might be helpful to you.

Questions to Consider

For becoming a caregiver:
- Do I have the physical strength to do this?

- Do I have the psychological strength to sustain me through the stress of caregiving?
- How can I balance taking care of my loved one and taking care of myself?
- Can I be gentle with the one to whom I am giving care?
- How can I balance my concern for safety with the importance of honoring my loved one's desire for independence?

For becoming a caregetter:
- How can I deal with the guilt I feel that my needs will require my caregiver to give up time and energy to take care of me?
- Is there any other way I can manage without making demands on my loved ones?
- How can I acknowledge my anger at the situation that sometimes might manifest as resentment toward those who are helping me?
- How can I cultivate gratitude in the face of the challenges I'm facing?
- How do I hold on to the truth that I am still the same person even as I need more care?

The Gathering
Time and Place
This ritual can take place in your home, whenever it feels right or at a time when family or close friends customarily gather.

People
Include family and close friends, and the person who is caregiving and/or the person who is caregetting.

Materials
Wide ribbon
Permanent markers or cloth markers

Ritual[2]
A witness/friend offers this intention as a meditation: "It's like this now."

Caregiver says:
> Source of all life, help me to care for my loved one, with hope, courage, and sensitivity. Grant me insight, resourcefulness, and the ability to ask for help and to accept help when it is needed. May I find the patience to overcome difficult moments and to find meaning and purpose in the smallest task. Help me to remember to take care of myself so that I may have the strength to help others. Be with me and my loved one as we journey on this path together. May the future bring many occasions for joy and connection.

Caregetter says:
> I hoped this moment would never come. May I discover the strength to be present to this moment that acknowledges a transition in my life as my ability to be engaged in the world has begun to change. May I and my caregiver focus on what I can do instead of what I can no longer do, and may I be optimistic and attentive to the joy present in my life even as difficulties exist. May I be grateful to be loved and clear that I am worthy of the love I get, and may I find pleasure and light even when my situation feels uncertain and dark.[3]

Participants together might read or sing the *Mi Shebeirach* prayer for healing.[4]

Next, either or both the caregiver and caregetter recite:
> Blessed is the Eternal One, who gives me the ability to remember those blessings that are still mine to affirm and the strength to arise anew each day.[5]

Participants then write one word of blessing for the caregiver and/or caregetter on the ribbons using the markers. These one-word blessings may be shared toward the end of the ritual.

A participant reads this poem:

> *Jacob was left alone. And a man (angel) wrestled*
> *with him until the break of dawn.*
> —Genesis 32:25

It found me dipping my toes in the river.
"No, I'm not ready," I pleaded. "Too soon."

It laughed
and bared its teeth.
"Ready or not, here I come."
And grabbed me.

I held on. And on. And on.
It grew stronger
I more determined.

When dawn broke it loosened its grip.
We sank down by the river's bank.
Exhausted, we tossed pebbles into the water.
Debated life and death.
Agreed to disagree.

"You took too much," I complained.
"At least, give me a blessing."

It rose to leave
then sighed
turned back
handed me a bouquet of memories.

Cradling it in shaky hands
I rose too.
And limped away.[6]
—Rabbi Debra R. Hachen

Next, those gathered offer their words of blessing to the caregiver and/or caregetter.

All recite the *Shehecheyanu*:

בָּרוּךְ אַתָּה, יְיָ, אֱלֹהֵינוּ מֶלֶךְ הָעוֹלָם,
שֶׁהֶחֱיָנוּ וְקִיְּמָנוּ וְהִגִּיעָנוּ לַזְּמַן הַזֶּה.

*Baruch atah, Adonai, Eloheinu Melech haolam,
shehecheyanu v'kiy'manu v'higianu laz'man hazeh.*

We praise You, *Adonai* our God, Sovereign of the universe, whose nurturance of us as we travel through life has brought us to this particular time and this particular place. Amen.[7]

Ruth's Story

"Being a caregiver for someone you love is a complicated and challenging situation. In my case my husband, Richard, was terminally ill with ALS (amyotrophic lateral sclerosis). Receiving the diagnosis was a horrible shock. Although he and I both struggled with grief, we didn't dwell on it or talk about it much; there was so much to learn about ALS so that I could help him and take care of him. I tried to make each day as pleasant as possible—welcoming friends and family for visits even though I was tired and had an overwhelming amount of work to do. Even with a home health aide coming several days a week, my job was enormous. It involved taking care of his declining condition, ordering and keeping track of the medications, getting him to appointments, making nourishing meals for him when he was losing weight and his ability to chew and swallow were declining, helping him get dressed and bathed, making sure he was safely navigating around the apartment, staying beside him when he took his medicine because of the danger of choking, and learning to administer nourishment through the feeding tube. I was exhausted most of the time. I felt I was living in an endless nightmare, wondering how much longer I could sustain myself, hoping I wouldn't get sick myself, wanting him to live but also fearing that he could need my care for years or that, despite his illness, he could outlive me. It was impossible and confusing to figure out what I wished for. We were together for fifty-eight years, and I didn't want to lose him, but the prospect of his future decline in functioning was scary. As time went on, I felt more and more loneliness because Richard couldn't speak and his communication through typing phrases was nothing like having a conversation with him.

"I found I was the recipient of well-meaning but often annoying advice from people: 'You have to get more help' was the constant refrain from friends and relatives. I was advised to keep my life going and get out more, although I had no desire to do so and said so. I just wanted to be with Richard, help him as much as I could, and make sure he knew I would always be there for him.

"I survived the ordeal of caregiving by keeping my own counsel and using my own brand of self-care—simple pleasures, ordering in Chinese food and other treats, listening to music, crying in private when I needed to, talking with family and friends who were caring and sympathetic, and putting one foot in front of the other to get everything done. Visits from family and friends were wonderful and made our days seem more normal and bearable. One of Richard's old friends from medical school came to visit on a regular basis to play chess with him when Richard could no longer speak. Visits with our adult son were particularly poignant, as he asked many questions, wanting to know more of his dad's thinking, knowing that Richard was terminal.

"The ALS Association lent us equipment and allowed us to attend ALS support groups online. We learned from others who were experiencing similar issues. Being part of the Chai Village synagogue community and receiving calls and visits from Chai Village friends was a bedrock that sustained me and enabled me to keep going.

"I knew I was losing Richard, and I wanted to honor him while he was alive and express my gratitude to him for the years we spent together. I hope my experiences and thoughts will help others choose the caregiving path that is right for them."

Alissa's Story
"I had been sleeping in another room for four years since my husband got too seriously ill to share a bed. After he died, I bought a new bed, but I still wasn't ready to make the move back to the room we had shared for so many years. Finally, just before the unveiling, I was ready. I felt like I needed to say a prayer to mark this moment. I really didn't know what was appropriate, but what came to mind was the *Shehecheyanu*. It felt good to say it, so I guess it was right even if there might have been something else that would have been better. What did matter was that taking that moment to say a prayer was meaningful. It helped me touch the gratitude for our life together, the sadness that we didn't get to grow old together, and the blessing of knowing that what he wanted for me was to move forward in my life."

For Clergy: Adapting for Communal Settings
Create a service to honor and bless caregivers, modeled on this one shared by Rabbi Paul Kipnes, spiritual leader of Congregation Or Ami in Calabasas, California:

> Every few years, we invite congregants and community members who are or have been caretakers for loved ones to a special Friday night service. The service integrates prayers of healing with caregivers' first-person reflections on current or previous experiences. The theme of the service is the holiness of helping and the *k'dushah* [holiness] of caretaking. We open with the story of someone who is currently caregiving, and they share their reflections upon the joys and challenges, the exhaustion and the meaning of setting aside sacred time to take care of loved ones. It is followed by songs, and then we have a speaker talk about five lessons learned while lovingly caring for a parent. That is followed by the naming of loved ones for whom we are caring. Congregants currently caregiving are invited up to the bimah, where they gather before the ark and are wrapped in tallitot. Each caregiver shares the

name of their loved one and their relationship to them, and one sentence about the experience—positive, negative, or neutral.

I give them this blessing: "*Makor hachayim*, Source of life, who is with us through our joys and sorrows, grant strength and courage, patience and compassion to these holy helpers who are taking care of their loved ones. Be with them through the sadness and the exhaustion, remind them of the love, and show them solace. Allow them to remember the person who was, amidst the confusion that is. Suffuse their souls with the sense that because of this holy work, they are helping their loved one to move from this moment to whatever comes next. *Baruch atah, Adonai, shomei-a t'filah*. Blessed are You, *Adonai*, who hears our prayers."

Words of Wisdom

We are inextricably connected—with each other, with our communities, with our Earth, and with God. What each of us does makes a difference for the other. This truth becomes more apparent as we grow older. The work of wise aging involves coming to see ourselves from this larger perspective. As the generations that came before cared for us, so we care for the next. And as the generations before us received support from others, so can we receive support. Our ability to model that for the next generation can be one of the most powerful aspects of our legacy.[8]
—*Rabbi Rachel Cowan and Dr. Linda Thal*

CHAPTER 16
Starting or Ending Medical Treatment

> You turned my mourning into dancing,
> so that my soul will sing to you and it not be still.[1]
> —Debbie Friedman (*based on Psalm 30:12*)

Introduction

In *Illness as Metaphor*, Susan Sontag writes, "Illness is the night side of life, a more onerous citizenship. Everyone who is born holds dual citizenship, in the kingdom of the well and in the kingdom of the sick. Although we all prefer to use the good passport, sooner or later each of us is obliged, at least for a spell, to identify ourselves as citizens of that other place."[2] No one wants to enter that land, but many of us will. And as we enter, we hope that we will return to the land of the well. Our lives change as we enter and the lives of people we love change as well. Finding a way to mark this transition in the presence of those people can help make the challenges a bit easier. Celebrating with those people when we return to health makes that reentry more joyful.

There are wonderful resources in *On the Doorposts of Your House* (CCAR Press) and in *Mishkan R'fuah* (CCAR Press) for beginning, undergoing, and concluding medical treatment. Any of those readings can be incorporated into a ritual you might choose to create as you face surgery, heart disease, or chronic illness. We focus here on a ritual for beginning chemotherapy.[3] Several of the stories relate to cancer. The questions to consider are relevant for other illnesses, as in one of the stories and some additional sidebars.

Questions to Consider

- Who are the people who can be a part of your support system as you begin this journey?

- Are there other times in your life when you faced difficult challenges that might offer insight as to how to face this one?

The Gathering

Time and Place

Hold this ritual in a place where you feel comfortable, such as your home or at the home of a friend, after a decision to cut your hair before or during chemotherapy.

People

Invite friends and family.

Materials

A haircutting tool (scissors or razor)
A haircutting cape
Wine or grape juice
Spices
Braided candle
Matches

Ritual

Gather family/friends in a circle, with the person about to undergo chemotherapy sitting in the center. This person explains what this moment means to them and why they decided to mark it with ritual. Next, this person reads the *Asher Yatzar* prayer:

> Praise to You, *Adonai* our God, Sovereign of the universe, who formed the human body with skill, creating the body's many pathways and openings. It is well known before Your throne of glory that if one of them be wrongly opened or closed, it would be impossible to endure and stand before You. Blessed are You, *Adonai*, who heals all flesh, working wondrously.[4]

A friend or family member places the haircutting cape around the subject and begins the cutting or shaving as those assembled sing a song or a *nigun* that has some meaning to the person getting their hair cut.

When the haircutting is complete, a friend explains why the ceremony will end with the symbols of *Havdalah* even though it is not necessarily a Saturday evening. They might choose this reading:

> We will end the ritual with a brief *Havdalah* ceremony because *Havdalah* acknowledges separations and distinctions, like *kodesh* (holy) from *chol* (mundane), and light from dark. Beginning chemotherapy is also a kind of separation—a transition from normal life to the months of chemo. Chemo separates the dangerous cancer cells from the otherwise healthy body. And *Havdalah* highlights multiple senses—taste of the wine, smell of the spices, touch and warmth of the fire. Chemo can affect several senses: sight, taste, and touch. May this *Havdalah* ceremony bode well for your senses remaining intact, and may you remember that any effects on your body are likely only temporary.

Finally, the ritual facilitator pours a glass of wine, lights the candle, and leads the group in the *Havdalah* blessings:

בָּרוּךְ אַתָּה, יְיָ, אֱלֹהֵינוּ מֶלֶךְ הָעוֹלָם, בּוֹרֵא פְּרִי הַגָּפֶן.
Baruch atah, Adonai, Eloheinu Melech haolam, borei p'ri hagafen.
Blessed are You, Source of life and all Creation—
You create the fruit of the vine.

בָּרוּךְ אַתָּה, יְיָ, אֱלֹהֵינוּ מֶלֶךְ הָעוֹלָם, בּוֹרֵא מִינֵי בְשָׂמִים.
Baruch atah, Adonai, Eloheinu Melech haolam, borei minei v'samim.
Blessed are You, Source of life and all Creation—
You create the varied spices.

בָּרוּךְ אַתָּה, יְיָ, אֱלֹהֵינוּ מֶלֶךְ הָעוֹלָם, בּוֹרֵא מְאוֹרֵי הָאֵשׁ.
Baruch atah, Adonai, Eloheinu Melech haolam, borei m'orei ha-eish.
Blessed are You, Source of life and all Creation—
You create the fire's light.

Extinguish the candle in the wine glass and conclude with a song, perhaps "Ozi V'zimrat Yah," or any other music that feels appropriate.

Sarah's Story

"Rather than wait for my hair to fall out, I decided to cut it short. I chose to do this haircut in my backyard, surrounded by my husband, teenage children, and a few close friends, which I called my 'pre-chemo *opshern*,' inspired by the Chasidic *upsherinish* (Yiddish for haircut), when a three-year-old boy celebrates his first haircut surrounded by family and friends, incorporating blessings, songs, and Torah study.

"The *opshern* began with refreshments and upbeat music. The guests sat in a circle of chairs, and I explained why I decided to cut my hair. After a brief recitation, guests were asked to study some texts and reflect on the question: What do hair and haircutting represent in the Jewish tradition, and how could that be useful for me today?

"Then the ritual haircut began. I donned a haircutting cape and moved my chair to the middle of the circle. My daughter put my hair into twelve ponytails, all at least eight inches long (the minimum required for donation). Each guest approached me and shared impromptu words. As my daughter did some final snips, someone brought me a mirror. I cringed, barely recognizing myself with short hair. But I stayed strong, thinking about the special words my friends and family had just shared. I was further bolstered when we sang two songs I find meaningful about personal strength and getting out of a narrow place: 'Ozi V'Zimrat Yah' (from Psalm 118:14) and 'Min HaMeitzar' (from Psalm 118:5).

"The *opshern* made the idea of starting chemo a little easier to swallow, and the participants' blessings have resonated in my head, bringing me strength during the difficult treatments. But I was not the only one standing on the precipice of changes. My family and friends now see me with an altered appearance and are vicariously experiencing some of the effects of chemo. Every one of the guests told me that they, too, found the ritual deeply meaningful at this moment of transition."

Bluma's Story

"In August 2022, at the age of forty-four, I was diagnosed with stage 2 invasive lobular carcinoma. A double mastectomy, three corrective surgeries, and thirty rounds of radiation later, I'm nearing the finish line in my treatment plan, which will ultimately take nine full months to complete. This week I met with my breast surgeon for a six-month follow-up visit. The visit went well and she declared me healthy, though it's still difficult to think of myself as being cancer-free. During my radiation treatments I cut large holes in a handful of shirts to allow my armpits to breathe during the most painful parts of treatment. Though they brought me comfort at the time, I knew I could never wear them again. But simply throwing them out didn't feel like an appropriate response to what I'd been through. So instead of burning bread for the pre-Passover ritual of *biur chameitz*, I set fire to what I call my 'radiation shirts.' The tradition of burning leavened bread before Passover symbolizes that we're getting rid of every last bit of leavening. The symbolism was clear. And just like we say a prayer for the bread we burn, I said a prayer declaring my house free of cancer, for today, and hopefully for forever: 'All cancer or anything cancer-related that is in my possession, whether I have seen it or not, whether I have observed it or not, whether I have removed it or not, shall be considered nullified and ownerless as the dust of the earth.'"[5]

Cyndi's Story

"I'm a potter. I work with clay. Fifteen years ago my doctor told me I had Parkinson's. I don't remember anything from that meeting. I don't remember the ride home with my husband. I don't remember what we talked about. But I do remember that later that day my husband drove me to my ceramic studio. I remember the light in the room, the feel of the piece I was working on, the moist clay, the confirmation that I was alive and that I am a potter. I feel most alive when I am creative.

"Shortly after, I began spending time at Wellness Works, a project of Boston's Beth Israel Hospital, which offers movement classes and educational/support programs designed to help those with Parkinson's live a healthy life. I realized how grateful I was for the community gathered there. I wanted to give back in some way, but it was not clear how. I knew that I loved to create, share, sell, and give away my work. I came up with an idea of reaching out to other artists with Parkinson's to share our art, sell it, and give the money to Wellness Works. The director was intrigued, and she and her colleague immediately got behind the project, reaching out to many who were already connected to Wellness Works and through them to others. We had no idea whether other people would come to the first meeting. Forty people did, and the group began to meet regularly, sharing our work, sharing the joy we felt through our work, and encouraging each other as our work began to change as our bodies were changing.

"I didn't actually create a ritual, though in some ways that first sale was a ritual because it marked a transition in my life and it created a community, diverse in so many ways but with two things in common—we are all artists and we all have Parkinson's. There are moments of transition and change in this journey; all that is easier with each other's support.

"As my Parkinson's has advanced, I can no longer work with clay. Yet I continue to be joyful knowing that so many friends think of me every day as they use the beautiful creations I have made."

For Clergy: Adapting for Communal Settings

For a person about to begin a treatment for a serious illness, it might be appropriate to share a private blessing from a clergyperson in front of the ark, such as this Prayer for One Approaching Surgery or Crisis:

God, You are with me in my moments of strength and of weakness. You know the trembling of my heart as the moments pass.

Grant wisdom and skill to the mind and hands of those whose lives touch mine.

Grant that I may return to fullness of life and wholeness of strength, not for my sake alone but also for those around me. Enable me to complete my days on earth with dignity and purpose. May I awaken to know the depth of Your healing power now and evermore. Amen.[6]

After treatment—for example, at the conclusion of radiation, chemotherapy, or recovery from surgery—invite the person for an *aliyah* to the Torah where they recite *Birkat HaGomeil*, the traditional prayer said upon successfully navigating a difficult journey, whether physical, spiritual, or emotional:

בָּרוּךְ אַתָּה, יְיָ, אֱלֹהֵינוּ מֶלֶךְ הָעוֹלָם,
הַגּוֹמֵל לְחַיָּבִים טוֹבוֹת שֶׁגְּמָלַנִי כָּל טוֹב.

*Baruch atah, Adonai, Eloheinu Melech haolam,
hagomeil l'chayavim tovot, sheg'malani kol tov.*

My thanks to You, Source of life and all Creation,
who in Your inscrutable way watches over the worthy and the
wayward, for having graciously given me abundant kindness
by shielding me from great harm.[7]

Words of Wisdom

From the narrow place I called to You:
You answered me from a place of expansiveness.

—Psalm 118:5

PART FOUR
Community

CHAPTER 17

Saying Goodbye to a Parent's Home

> In many houses
> all at once
> I see my mother and father
> and they are young
> as they walk in.
>
> Why should my
> tears come,
> to see them laughing?
>
> That they cannot
> see me
> is of no matter.
>
> I was once
> their dream;
> now
> they are mine.[1]
> —Diane Cole

Introduction

CLEANING OUT a parent's home is a chore (the same can be said for any beloved person's home—whether it is the home of a parent, another family member, or a friend). A ritual that marks this transition can turn this chore into a sacred act. Your parents might still be alive and preparing to move to a senior care facility, or this cleaning might occur after their death. Here we offer a prayer to begin the process, one that you might say each time you enter to do the work of sorting, discarding, recycling, saving, and remembering.

Questions to Consider
- If your parent(s) is (are) still alive, how can you prepare with them for this moment?
- What are some memories you have associated with this home or these things?
- Who are the people you want to share these memories with?
- How do you choose what to keep and what to discard as you are confronted with all that your parent(s) saved?
- How do you think you'll feel when some of these things are relocated to your home?

The Gathering

Time and Place

Whenever you are ready to begin, conduct this ritual at your parents' home.

People

This ritual can be done alone, with friends or family members, or with those helping you clean.

Materials

A candle
A soundtrack of music that is or might have been meaningful to your parents
A tool for removing a mezuzah
Materials (like trash bags) for cleaning the house

Ritual

As you enter the home, stop for a few moments of quiet, and perhaps take a deep breath. Say this:

> Source of compassion, as we enter the home of our beloved parents, [if the parents have died] who have left us to be closer to You / [or, if they are moving to a senior living facility] who have made the decision to move to a senior living facility, please guide our actions to be in accordance with Jewish tradition, as well as in accordance with their wishes. Help us to move through their

home, which so enriched our lives, in a manner that is a tribute to their teachings and their values. May we perform this poignant and sad duty with reverence and with dignity.

May we do so with generosity to others in the family, acknowledging their desire for some of these mementos, and with generosity to others in the community who might benefit from these possessions.[2]

When the cleaning is completely finished and the home is empty, light the candle. With very close family and/or friends, go from room to room, sit quietly, and share a memory from that room that brought joy to those present or to your parent(s), thank the room, and move on to the next one. After being in each room, thank each other, and if the parents are dead, recite *Kaddish*. If the new family who will inhabit the home in the future is not Jewish, remove the mezuzah. At the end of the ritual, blow out the candle. Conclude your time together with a meal at a parent's favorite restaurant and share more stories.

As Is

Objects new to this place, I receive you.
It was I who sent for each of you.
The house of my mother is empty.
I have emptied it of all her things.
The house of my mother is sold with
All its trees and their usual tall music.
I have sold it to the stranger,
The architect with three young children.

Things of the house of my mother,
You are many. My house is
Poor compared to yours and hers.
My poor house welcomes you.
Come to rest here. Be at home. Please
Do not be frantic do not
Fly whistling up out of your places.

You, floor- and wall-coverings, be
Faithful in flatness; lie still;
Try. By light or by dark
There is no going back.
You, crystal bowls, electrical appliances,
Velvet chair and walnut chair,
You know your uses; I wish you well.
My mother instructed me in
 your behalf.

I have made room for you. Most of you
Knew me as a child; you can tell
We need not be afraid of each other.

And you, old hopes of the house of
 my mother,
Farewell.[3]
—*Marie Ponsot*

Nomi's Story

"Two months before my father passed away, my hands began making spiral-shaped objects from wire. Some became beads; others small spheres. One particularly organic shape looked like a cyclone. When I covered it with translucent polymer clay, the cyclone transformed into a chrysalis. It was both strong and delicate, a shape for becoming. Drawn to this form, I made more of them.

"I made chrysalises almost obsessively right up until my father's death. These chrysalises were, I believe, a communication from deep within or perhaps beyond me that a time of transformation was coming—certainly for my father, but also for me. (As a caregiver, my life was bound to change dramatically once my father passed.) A few months after my father's death, I set back to making more of these odd little forms—my hands working away without much thinking. I never chose to make the chrysalises; they chose me.

"Other forms sprang into being as well: spiral shell shapes. I covered these, too, with translucent polymer clay. As I continued to make the forms, I simultaneously began emptying out my childhood home in preparation to sell the house. The grief and resistance that came with this task were immense, but a vision began forming that helped me press forward. Perhaps I wasn't going toward emptiness and loss but rather toward transformation. I would not be emptying the home of all signs of life, but instead preparing it for new life. I would transform it into a gallery space to house—if temporarily—these

---

If at all possible, begin the task of sorting with your parents before they are ready to move. As you look at the furniture or other treasures, take photographs, and ask your parents to tell stories about the memories the pieces evoke in them. Video their responses or write them down. Perhaps play some of their favorite music as you go through this work. Reward yourselves as each day's work is finished with their favorite takeout food. Encourage them to begin sending some of what they are prepared to let go of to the people who might welcome it.

spiral forms that my hands were bringing forth. And so, my childhood bedroom became a gallery, and perhaps a springboard for my new life. A cocoon of possibility."

Mark's Story

"Leaving my parents' home was made more difficult because of the wonderful garden in the back and the trees alongside the house. I have so many memories of working in the garden, pulling weeds, and harvesting the vegetables. I knew that bringing some seeds from the garden to my home would be meaningful. I didn't anticipate that the new owners would want the Japanese maple under which my son's foreskin had been planted thirty years prior to be cut down because they were concerned it would fall. So after it had been cut, I took several of its branches, with the plan of repurposing the wood, maybe even as chuppah poles for my son's upcoming wedding."

For Clergy: Adapting for Communal Settings

Clergy may invite those in the community who recently went through this process for a special group blessing or *aliyah* for the Torah reading.

Words of Wisdom

Memory is the past as present, as it lives on in me.
Without memory there can be no identity.[4]
— *Rabbi Jonathan Sacks*

CHAPTER 18

Decluttering or Downsizing Your Home

An American visitor was passing through the Polish town of Radim and stopped in to visit the Chafetz Chayim. Entering the great sage's simple apartment, he was struck by how sparsely it was furnished. "Where is your furniture?" the man asked.

"Where is yours?" replied the Chafetz Chayim.

"Oh, I am only passing through," answered the man.

"I too am only passing through," was the Chafetz Chayim's reply.[1]

—*Alan Morinis*

Introduction

WE NEVER REALLY needed all of it. However, we all tend to accumulate stuff over the years for different reasons. Most of it holds some kind of meaning, like school trophies, party dresses, the desk chair with your grandfather's college insignia on the back. At some point, decluttering has to be done, whether your pending move is in the distant future or is coming up much sooner. This ritual is designed to capture the wealth of emotions involved during this process and to make the most of the opportunities for generosity, connection, and legacy it offers.

Questions to Consider

- What are some memories you have associated with this home or these things?
- Who are the people you want to share these memories with?
- How do you choose what to keep and what to discard as you are confronted with all that you have saved?
- How do you feel if your loved ones—kids, if you have them, or your family of choice—don't want your stuff? Is it the thing itself you care about, or is it the story connected to the thing? How can you preserve the story, if not the thing?

The Gathering

Time and Place

This ritual can be held whenever you give things away (over a period of time), or whenever you are thinking about downsizing or are cleaning out your home in preparation for a move.

People

Invite the people to whom you'd like to leave your stuff, even though they may not want it.

Materials

A camera with a video function

Ritual

The person who is decluttering or preparing to move begins by saying:

> I have in my home treasures that matter to me. They connect me to people I loved, to memories that have shaped the person I have become. While I'd love to have these treasures be part of your homes now, I know that is not what you want. And as much as I love having these treasures, especially the ones that were in the home of my (grandparents/parents/beloved friends), what really matters to me is not the object, but the person connected to it.
>
> I invite you to walk with me around the house so I can tell you their stories, take a photograph of each treasure, and tell you what I know about its history and about the person who gave it to me. I hope you will share with me any associations you have with this piece or with the person connected to it.

Next, do exactly that—walk around the house, talk about the items in your home that have meaning, and record your stories for posterity.

End with these words:

> With gratitude for the abundance of my life, I honor those who came before me and those who will come after me as I move forward into the future—with less baggage.

Laura's Story

"When my grandmother was about to leave her apartment to move to a senior living facility, all of her grandchildren and her two daughters met to divide up her treasures—some antique furniture, some serving dishes, a set of silver, jewelry, and the paintings that adorned her walls. The grandchildren, all now adults with families of our own, knew the stories we had heard from our mothers of how our grandmother would tape the name of one of them to the bottom of a piece of furniture to designate which daughter should get it when she died and how she would change the designation when she was angry with one or the other. We drew lots to determine an order and then, in order, we chose what we wanted until everything was spoken for. It was a poignant, fun, and mildly stressful way for siblings and cousins to bond, tell stories of our growing up with these grandparents, and admit to ourselves and each other that one day we would each reenact some version of this with our own parents, ourselves, and our children. The best of my treasures was my grandmother's antique breakfront, which I had shipped from Boston to Los Angeles, where it now graces my living room. My children grew up in my home with that breakfront. And when the time comes for me to downsize, I will be faced with the painful truth: My kids don't want it. In fact, my kids don't really want any of my stuff. They have their own unique aesthetic, different from mine, and they don't have much room for more stuff in the homes they have."

Caroline's Story

"Samuel and I decided it was time to leave Los Angeles in July 2022, following a year traveling by pickup truck, during which we visited our grown children in Columbus, Ohio, and Weston, Connecticut. It was a big decision, as we had lived for many decades in LA. That July, Samuel made a gut decision that at 10 a.m. on October 27, we would be packed and pulling out of the driveway. Between July and October we had a lot to do!

"After so many decades in Los Angeles, we looked around our two-thousand-square-foot condo and realized we had accumulated an enormous pile of possessions. We made lists of rooms, closets, and storage areas. An important ritual was actually touching each possession and deciding 'yes or no,' 'stay or go.'

"This took time and emotional energy. Ultimately, it was quite satisfying to have a full grasp on our worldly belongings."

For Clergy: Adapting for Communal Settings
Clergy could identify a few members of the congregation who are in the process of downsizing and bring them together. Once or several times a year the group could organize a flea market fundraiser or a giveaway. A variation of this for Jewish communities would be to collect Judaica (candlesticks, mezuzot, *Kiddush* cups, challah covers, *chanukiyot*) and gift them to students in an Introduction to Judaism program for potential converts or to college students through a local Hillel.

Words of Wisdom

Abundance
Two perspectives govern our way
Of seeing the world: abundance and scarcity.
These perspectives are a choice.
The cup is not half empty,
Nor is it half full.
Rather our cup runneth over,
overflowing.[2]
—*Rabbi Karyn Kedar*

CHAPTER 19

Leaving Your Home

A house is built by wisdom, and is established by understanding; by knowledge are its rooms filled with all precious and beautiful things.[1]
—*Proverbs 24:3–4*

Introduction

AMONG THE PLACES some of us remember is the home where we grew up or the home where we raised our children, if we had children. We have memories of celebrations, events, and gatherings where we cultivated friendships and connections. Leaving that home as we move onto the next stage of our lives is bittersweet—there is excitement about what might lay ahead and also sadness that we are leaving behind what was so important—the place, the friends, and the life we lived there. Marking this moment both acknowledges this ambivalence and gives us an opportunity to look back over our lives in that particular place and to thank some of those people who have been so central in our lives.

Questions to Consider
- What are the reasons you are moving?
- Have you made a major move at other times in your life? Is there anything you learned through that experience that might be helpful to you now?
- Are there specific people in your life now whom you want to thank?
- Are there people in your life now with whom you want to devote effort to maintaining your relationship?

The Gathering[2]

Time and Place
Hold this ritual when the move is imminent, ideally when the house is almost empty, at your home.

People
Include close friends and family in the neighborhood or community you are leaving.

Materials
If you have a mezuzah on a door of your home, a tool to remove it

For those who are moving, an object you would like to take from this home that captures the joy this place brought to you

A playlist of some favorite songs or songs connected to the years lived in the house

Wine or grape juice or champagne

Glasses

Ritual
As people gather, have the music playing in the background.

Participant or facilitator says:

> The Bible tells the story of God's call to Avram (Abraham) and Sarai (Sarah) with the words "Go, really go [*Lech l'cha*] from your land ... to a place that I will show you ... and you will be a blessing" (Genesis 12:1–2).[3] Abraham and Sarah were both in later midlife when they heard that invitation. They didn't know where they were going. You know the name of the place you are going and a number of important things about it. So we gather together to wish you the courage to make this move, the patience to give yourself all the time you need, and the curiosity to discover a new community. We're sad that you are leaving, but hopeful that you will come back often to visit and to continue to cherish the friendships you have made here.

Take a mezuzah off a door. (If there is a mezuzah on the front door and the house is being sold to a Jewish person, the tradition is to leave the mezuzah. If the new owner is not Jewish, one may take the mezuzah off. For this ceremony, if the front-door mezuzah is to remain, take down a mezuzah on a door within the house.)

The person or people moving then present an object that they want to bring to their new home and explain its significance.

With the playlist again in the background, give participants time to wander through the house and write down memories they have from spending time in it. Participants share those memories, using the mezuzah as a talking stick. Alternatively, those present may offer a simple blessing for the ones who are moving.

The person or people moving then recite the opening of the prayer *Mah Tovu* (Numbers 24:5):

מַה טֹּבוּ אֹהָלֶיךָ, יַעֲקֹב, מִשְׁכְּנֹתֶיךָ, יִשְׂרָאֵל.

Mah tovu ohalecha, Yaakov, mishk'notecha, Yisrael.

How goodly are your tents, O Jacob, your dwellings, O Israel.

Next, the person or people moving open the door or a window and say:
> May all that has blessed me here bless those who will inhabit the space after me.
> May all that has challenged me here be released.
> May all the good memories from this place go with me as I move forward in my life.

Householders thank those present for enriching their lives in this home. Then conclude with the words from the *Hashkiveinu* prayer:

וּשְׁמֹר צֵאתֵנוּ וּבוֹאֵנוּ לְחַיִּים וּלְשָׁלוֹם מֵעַתָּה וְעַד עוֹלָם.

Ushmor tzeiteinu uvo-einu l'chayim ulshalom, mei-atah v'ad olam.

Guard our going and coming to life and to peace evermore.

All gathered, pour wine or champagne into cups and drink a *l'chayim*—to life.

Conclude with a good nosh, preferably potluck.

Roz's Story

"After a relatively short illness my husband, Ted, died. I knew I wanted to leave the home we had shared and to downsize to a smaller apartment. It took some time to find the right new apartment and then to go through all of our stuff to decide what to bring with me to my new home. It was wise for me to move into the new place before I had to be completely out of the old one.

"With the help of good friends, I organized our books and donated most of his to the synagogue library. I figured I would probably never host a large seder again, so I gave away all my Passover dishes. I measured the new apartment to figure out what of my furniture would fit, and I gave away everything that wouldn't. I did all this quickly—maybe too quickly—because it was hard for me to stay in the home where we had been together for so long. I remember one particular pair of shoes—I can't find them, but I'd like them back. And I wish I still had those Passover dishes.

"When the house was empty, I invited my ten closest friends to come to the empty house on a Saturday evening and bring chairs and tissues. One woman brought her guitar. We sat in a circle in what had been the dining room. Everyone there was familiar with *Havdalah*, the ceremony that celebrates separation when we move from one spiritual place to another, saying goodbye to the joy and comfort of Shabbat and fortifying ourselves for the challenges of the coming week. It seemed like the perfect metaphor for bringing the sweetness of my life with Ted into my new life as a solo ager, with all the challenges that might bring. Before each of the blessings—over wine, over spices, over light—I asked my friends to share a memory they had of something that happened in our home. Before the final blessing, I passed around a plate that had bittersweet and milk chocolate pieces and almonds on it, remembering the sweet times, the difficult/bitter times, and the times Ted and I drove each other nuts in the forty years we spent together there. Then I thanked them for helping us during Ted's horrible final year and carrying me since his death. One of the friends had organized a potluck dinner at her home, which was nearby, and we all went there afterward. I hadn't really wanted to do that, but it turned out to be nice—and I'm certainly glad I didn't just have to return immediately to my new apartment alone."

Samuel's Story

"Our story is more about leaving a community than about leaving a home. We agreed that all we enjoyed about living in Los Angeles was pretty much 'replaceable,' except our friends, of course.

"We composed a list of all our favorite people and created a paper countdown calendar. Over a shared meal, we told each couple or individual that we were planning on leaving. That took time and many tears. We were both very touched by how deeply our friends were saddened by our decision to leave this community.

"As a send-off, we arranged for a big dinner party in a private room at a favorite restaurant. We invited everyone on our list, told stories, made jokes, took pictures, and promised this night was *au revoir*, not *adieu*. Again, there were tears all around.

"Now almost two full years later, we both can say we've kept our promise, with regular calls and occasional visits with our chosen family of friends from Los Angeles.

"In terms of what we would have done differently, I think a regret is that we didn't get a formal blessing and send-off from our temple. The timing just didn't work out. That being said, we treasure the Traveler's Prayer key chain that our rabbi gave us as we were about to move on to this new adventure."

For Clergy: Adapting for Communal Settings

In a place of worship or community center, clergy may invite the person about to move for a blessing. Include a prayer or song such as *T'filat Ha-Derech*, also known as the Traveler's Prayer:

> May you be blessed as you go on your way
> May you be guided in peace
> May you be blessed with health and joy
> May this be your blessing, amen.
> May you be sheltered by wings of peace
> May you be kept in safety and in love
> May grace and compassion find their way to every heart
> May this be your blessing, amen.
> Amen, may this be your blessing, amen.[4]

Or offer this blessing (this blessing assumes that a person has raised children in this home; it needs to be adapted for those who did not):

> When students complete a book of the Talmud
> They often linger and celebrate the fulfillment of their efforts
> In a lifetime filled with many chapters and completions.
> Like them, you linger and celebrate all you received in your house.
> As you close one chapter of your lives and begin another,
> You remember with gratitude the many blessings
> You enjoyed under the shelter of your roof.
> In this home, you built a haven from the outside world.
> Its walls protected you from the elements,
> Its light drove away the darkness that crouched at night,
> Its warmth nurtured your love and gave you proof against the cold.
> You remember with gratitude these many blessings.
> You celebrate with joy the family you built upon this foundation.
> Into this home, you poured your dreams and efforts.
> You shared your love and filled these rooms with youthful laughter
> And an argument or two along the way.
> You saw your children's feet slowly gain their footing
> As they learned, all too quickly, to call another place their home.

Across these floors you walked and ran and danced in equal measure.
You celebrate with joy the family you built upon this foundation.
You honor with affection all those who crossed this threshold with you
From the time you first turned the key in the lock until today.
Through these doors you brought your children
And welcomed your friends and family.
With those who crossed this doorway,
You celebrated your triumphs and joys and shared your sorrows and fears.
With them, you marked the holidays and the milestones of your lives.
They helped make this house your home.
You honor with affection all those who crossed this threshold with you.
Today, you close one chapter of your lives and begin another.
May it be Your will, *Adonai* our God, that just as You have helped them
Complete the chapter inscribed in the walls, foundation, and gates of this home,
You will help them to begin a new chapter in a new home.
When Jacob journeyed from Gilead, the angels of God encountered him.
When he saw them, Jacob said: "This is God's camp."
By leaving one home and making another we know we do not leave God.
As you begin a new chapter of your lives,
We pray that your new home will provide you with all the fulfillment
You enjoyed under the shelter of this roof and upon its foundation.
Kein y'hi ratzon . . . May this be God's will.[5]
—*Rabbi Michael Howald*

Words of Wisdom

Blessed shall you be in your comings
and blessed shall you be in your goings.
—*Deuteronomy 28:6 and Psalm 121:8*

CHAPTER 20

Moving into a New Community and a New Home

> If you want to talk about this
> come to visit. I live in the house
> near the corner, which I have named
> Gratitude.[1]
> —Mary Oliver

Introduction

YOU'VE DECIDED to move to a new community, spent time in that community, and done your research about what matters to you about where you live. Public transportation? Retail stores close enough that you can walk, plus cafés, bookstores, and restaurants? Cultural offerings? Recreational opportunities—public parks, golf, tennis, pickleball, a fitness center? A library? A religious community? If you are moving to be closer to people you love, you've asked them to host a meal or a gathering with some of their friends and share with you what they think about this community. If religious or cultural fellowship is important to you, you have visited the synagogues, churches, or community centers. You have decided whether to buy or rent or whether you are ready to move into a senior living facility. Now you are ready to move and to consecrate your new home.

Questions to Consider

- What excites you most about this transition to your new community and your new home?
- What makes you most anxious?

The Gathering[2]

Time and Place

This ritual can be held as you settle into your new home, at your new home.

People

Invite people you know in your new community, or people you've met and would like to know better.

Materials

A mezuzah (or pick one or two of the symbols from the sidebar that feel right to you)
A glass wrapped tightly in a cloth or plastic bag
A Bible or a book that you love
Bread and salt
Floating candles
Bowls of water

Ritual

Gather outside the front door of your new home.

If this is a Jewish home, a participant explains the tradition of putting up a mezuzah:

> The custom of putting a mezuzah on the doorpost of your house comes from from Deuteronomy 6:4–9 and 11:13–9.
>
> Hear, O Israel! The Eternal is our God, the Eternal alone. You shall love the Eternal your God with all your heart, with all your soul, and with all your might. Take to heart these instructions with which I charge you this day. Impress them upon your children. Recite them when you stay at home and when you are away, when you lie down and when you get up. Bind them as a sign on your hand and let them serve as a symbol on your forehead; inscribe them on the doorposts of your house and on your gates. (Deuteronomy 6:4–9)
>
> The word *mezuzah* means "doorpost." It is a small rectangular box with a parchment scroll rolled inside with these Biblical texts written by a scribe. The mezuzah is placed on the front door on

the right side as you enter, approximately one-third of the way down from the top of the doorpost. It is typically placed on an angle facing toward the house, high enough so that someone touching it needs to be standing upright when they enter. It is slanted because of a compromise between those who argued it should be vertical and those who argued it should be horizontal. This compromise reminds the inhabitants of a home of the need to be willing to compromise for there to be *sh'lom bayit*, "peace in a home."

The mezuzah is placed with this blessing:

בָּרוּךְ אַתָּה, יְיָ, אֱלֹהֵינוּ מֶלֶךְ הָעוֹלָם,
אֲשֶׁר קִדְּשָׁנוּ בְּמִצְוֹתָיו וְצִוָּנוּ לִקְבֹּעַ מְזוּזָה.

*Baruch atah, Adonai, Eloheinu Melech haolam,
asher kid'shanu b'mitzvotav v'tzivanu likboa mezuzah.*

Blessed are You, Source of life and all Creation—
You have made us holy through connections,
to each other and to You, through placing the mezuzah.

בָּרוּךְ אַתָּה, יְיָ, אֱלֹהֵינוּ מֶלֶךְ הָעוֹלָם,
שֶׁהֶחֱיָנוּ וְקִיְּמָנוּ וְהִגִּיעָנוּ לַזְּמַן הַזֶּה.

*Baruch atah, Adonai, Eloheinu Melech haolam,
shehecheyanu v'kiy'manu v'higianu laz'man hazeh.*

Blessed are You, Source of life and all Creation—
You have kept us in life, sustained us,
and brought us to this moment of a new beginning.

The homeowners lead friends and family into the new home. As they step over the threshold, they step on a glass (wrapped in a cloth napkin or bag, so there are no dangerous shards). This symbolizes that they are moving forward in their lives with the knowledge that there will be brokenness and wholeness ahead, which they will face with courage and resilience, supported by the community around them.

The homeowners say:

A home is built by wisdom and established by understanding (Proverbs 24:3).
Welcome to our (my) new home.

A guest holds the Bible or another cherished book and expresses personal wishes that this home be filled with learning, with traditions that bring meaning, and with the expansiveness that comes from curling up in a comfortable chair exploring the world through reading.

Each person then lights a floating candle and places it in a bowl of water. As the candle is placed, they offer a one-sentence blessing: "May this home be filled with [one-word blessing]."

After each person has spoken, the homeowners share a few words about their hopes for this new sanctuary and their gratitude to all who have participated in this housewarming.

Bringing bread and salt signifies hospitality. According to Russian Jewish tradition, bread ensures there would always be enough food, and salt brings flavor to life. A guest offers bread and salt, expressing personal wishes for a home filled with good food, meals with friends and family, and just enough spice to keep life interesting. It is passed out to everyone present, with them breaking the bread together (with a blessing if that feels appropriate).

The ceremony concludes with a good meal and lots of toasts.

> There are a number of different rituals and traditions that you might want to incorporate into a ceremony for consecrating your new home:
> - Burning sage is a Native American tradition that is believed to remove bad energy from your home.
> - Planting an orange tree is a symbol of luck in China, because the words for "luck" and for "orange" sound similar in Chinese.
> - Scattering coins is a Filipino custom thought to bring prosperity to those who live in the house.
> - Boiling milk to overflowing evokes abundance and prosperity in Hindu homes.
> - Ringing a Tibetan bell to remove negative chi is a feng shui technique.
> - Lighting candles is the origin of the word "housewarming."

> For those who are moving into assisted living, an adaptation for this ritual could include putting up a mezuzah, words from the person moving, and this poem:
>
> **A Prayer for Entering Assisted Living**
> Today I may feel some ambivalence.
> I don't want to lose my autonomy.
> It's not easy to accept care.
>
> Help me, God, to see this change
> not as a diminishment in circumstance
> but simply my next chapter.
>
> Cultivate in me gratitude
> for those who prepare meals
> and keep track of medications.
>
> Open me to friendships
> with the other residents, each one
> a unique reflection of You.
>
> Attune me to unexpected blessings
> and awaken me to Your presence
> here and everywhere, now and always.[3]
> —*Rabbi Rachel Barenblat*

Susan and Yair's Story

Susan found COVID to be a very sobering reminder that the future is not guaranteed and one's time is not infinite. It rocked the way she and Yair were living their lives. While in their minds they always envisioned themselves in later years doing more outdoorsy adventures and living closer to nature than they did in Los Angeles, they figured they'd get around to that eventually. COVID was a strong incentive to take action—now.

For Yair, COVID had changed the dynamics of the entertainment industry. People preferred to just get on a Zoom or on a phone call rather than meet in person. Office days became less vital and his "office" became totally portable.

So they moved to Jackson, Wyoming, a place to which they both felt especially connected and knew well from spending vacations there. Yair explains, "COVID enabled me to have not only a more flexible and balanced work schedule, but also more time for 'play' in the beautiful mountains."

Becoming part of a new community has required them to really extend themselves to strangers and commit to building new relationships. They felt their move was like transferring to a new high school—to be happy, you have to set down new roots with new people. When they've made the effort, it has worked out. One example is that they have become good friends with their neighbors across the road after breaking bread together at their new home for Shabbat, Chanukah, the Super Bowl, and the Academy Awards.

Getting involved with civic action has also brought them into their new community. Yair recounted the second of two instances where they went to a hostage event in the town square organized by the two synagogues and three churches, "putting ourselves out there in a way that was a little awkward and uncomfortable." During that event, everyone stood outside in the middle of the town square chanting "Bring them home," and several people shared stories of recent trips to Israel or of having been in Israel on October 7. Yair, who was born and spent his early years in Israel, found this especially meaningful.

Susan's philosophy is that "wherever you unpack yourself, that's your home. In the process of moving from one place to another, I recognized that a lot of the things in the home we were living in are really not the core magic of what made it our home. It was the experiences we created in the house. It was sweet that after we moved in, the kids came up and we had the first of what I hope will be many family gatherings here. That made it a home."

CHAPTER 20: MOVING INTO A NEW COMMUNITY AND A NEW HOME

Bill and Lucy's Story

Bill and Lucy met through LinkedIn in 2001, four months after Bill was widowed. They clicked right away and were instantly comfortable. Bill moved from Delaware to Lucy's suburban Philadelphia home. They built a custom bedroom suite addition to the house. It was a space without a history, created just for them. Twelve years later, the youngest child had finally moved out, and they could think about downsizing. Bill was ready; Lucy was not. She still loved her house. She'd gone through a lot to keep it after her divorce, and Bill didn't press her.

One of their shared pastimes, however, had always been looking at homes for sale. Over the years, they saw their fair share of houses, but Lucy never wanted to do anything but look.

That changed when one day they walked into a model home fifteen minutes from where they lived, and Lucy literally said, "Wow!" It took another few months to say yes, put down the deposit, and begin the process of building the house. Eventually, they had a magnificent new home that was just for them. Every time they walk in the door, Lucy still says, "Wow!"

The best thing about their move was how warm and welcoming the new community turned out to be. Even though they hadn't consciously looked for it, it improved this next phase of their life immensely. That included the congregation whose services and events they began attending. The rabbi (also new, as they were) was dynamic and charismatic, and Lucy said, "Wow!" That first year, the rabbi was insistent that they were going to fill an entire truck with donated food for the Yom Kippur food drive. Lucy was intrigued; she calculated how many boxes they'd need (having just moved, she had all that information handy) and wrote a letter to the rabbi with the suggestion. She also enclosed a donation check to make it happen. Bill pointed out that if she wanted to be that involved with the food drive, they'd better join. Lucy agreed.

After the food drive, Bill and Lucy volunteered to work on the newsletter and building committee, attended the congregational second Passover seder, and participated in Torah study. They realized they'd jumped into the deep end—and did it gladly. Sometimes you find your community; sometimes your community finds you. But whichever it is, Bill and Lucy's advice is to always look for the "Wow!"

For Clergy: Adapting for Communal Settings

Once a year, organize an event and invite all new members or people who have recently moved to your community. Ask each to introduce themselves and say a word about who they are and their hopes for this new stage. Assign a congregation member to be a buddy to each relocated person and to commit to at least one shared meal or coffee over the next several months. Alternatively, you could cluster newly located people by zip code and have a member arrange at least one group meal over the next few months. For Jews, an ideal time for this would be during the holiday of Sukkot, the holiday where inviting guests is part of the tradition. For others, choose a time that might be meaningful to your community.

Words of Wisdom

A Blessing for the Home (*Birkat HaBayit*)

בְּזֶה הַשַּׁעַר לֹא יָבוֹא צַעַר.
בְּזֹאת הַדִּירָה לֹא תָבוֹא צָרָה.
בְּזֹאת הַדֶּלֶת לֹא תָבוֹא בֶּהָלָה.
בְּזֹאת הַמַּחְלָקָה לֹא תָבוֹא מַחְלוֹקֶת.
בְּזֶה הַמָּקוֹם תְּהִי בְרָכָה וְשָׁלוֹם.

May no sadness come through this gate.
May no trouble come to this dwelling.
May no fear come through this door.
May no conflict be in this place.
May this home be filled with blessing and peace.[4]

A Concluding Thought

All endings are beginnings. Doors close and doors can open if we make our days count and our moments matter. When we notice the joy and the sadness, the opportunity and the loss in the journey of growing older, we will travel the path with wisdom, curiosity, and grace.

> May the One who guides us through all the passages of our lives
> bless us with the strength to bear the labor pains of our own birth and rebirth;
> with the readiness to push when the moment is ripe,
> with a community to hold us and lift us up when we stumble on our way
> and celebrate with us as we continue to keep moving forward on our journey, wherever it might lead.[1]

Enjoy the journey.

Notes

Foreword
1. Mary Douglas, *Purity and Danger: An Analysis of Concepts of Pollution and Taboo* (Routledge, 2003), 65.
2. Stephanie Paulsell, *Religion Around Virginia Woolf* (Penn State University Press, 2020), 165.

Introduction
1. Dacher Keltner, preface to *The Power of Ritual: Turning Everyday Activities into Soulful Practices*, by Casper ter Kuile (HarperOne, 2021), x–xi.
2. Angeles Arrien, *The Second Half of Life: Opening the Eight Gates of Wisdom* (Sounds True, 2007), 4.

Chapter 1: Celebrating a Milestone Birthday
1. Dr. Bill Thomas, *Second Wind: Navigating the Passage to a Slower, Deeper, and More Connected Life* (Simon and Schuster, 2014), 210.
2. This ritual was first created for Barbara Balaban.

Chapter 2: Committing to a Purposeful New Focus
1. Reverend Howard Thurman, *The Living Wisdom of Howard Thurman: A Visionary for Our Time*, performed by Howard Thurman, audiobook (Sounds True, 2010).
2. Erik Erikson, *The Life Cycle Completed* (W. W. Norton, 1998), 4.
3. This blessing is from *The Book of Jewish Sacred Practices: CLAL's Guide to Everyday & Holiday Rituals & Blessings*, ed. Rabbi Irwin Kula and Vanessa L. Ochs, PhD (Jewish Lights, 2001), 201.
4. Debbie Friedman, "T'filat Haderech," track 12 on *You Shall Be a Blessing*, Sounds Write, 1997.
5. Adapted from "Setting Out on a Journey," in *L'chol Z'man V'Eit, For Sacred Moments: The CCAR Life-Cycle Guide*, ed. Rabbi Donald Goor (CCAR Press, 2015), Community-22.
6. SARK, "SARK's Newest Year Blessing, *SARK* (blog), https://www.planetsark.com/sarks-newest-year-blessing/.

Chapter 3: From Retirement to Renewment
1. Rabbi Ruth Sohn, "The Song of Miriam," originally published as "I Shall Sing to the Lord a New Song," in *Kol HaNeshamah: Shabbat VeHagim* (Reconstructionist Press, 2004), 769. Used by permission of the author.

2. This ritual is based on a ritual co-created by Rabbi Richard Camras and Rabbi Beth Lieberman in Los Angeles, 2021.
3. "For Retirement" from *To Bless the Space Between Us: A Book of Blessings* by John O'Donohue, copyright © 2008 by John O'Donohue, 167. Used by permission of Doubleday, an imprint of the Knopf Doubleday Publishing Group, a division of Penguin Random House LLC. All rights reserved.
4. Unpublished poem by Ronald M. Andiman, used with permission.
5. These blessings are adapted from Rabbi Ellen Weinberg Dreyfus's retirement ceremony.
6. Mary Oliver, "The Summer Day," in *Devotions: The Selected Poems of Mary Oliver* (Penguin Random House, 2017), 316.

Chapter 4: Embracing the Joy of Facing Finitude
1. Rabbi Rachel Cowan and Dr. Linda Thal, *Wise Aging: Living with Joy, Resilience, and Spirit* (Behrman House, 2015), 21.
2. *Mishkan HaNefesh: Machzor for the Days of Awe; Yom Kippur* (CCAR Press, 2015), 212.
3. Leonard Cohen, "Who by Fire?," track 11 on *The Essential Leonard Cohen*, Sound Ideas, 1974.
4. Rabbi Elana Zaiman, *The Forever Letter: Writing What We Believe for Those We Love* (Llewellyn Publications, 2017), 3–4.
5. Zaiman, *The Forever Letter*, 108.
6. Sam Levenson, "Ethical Will and Testament to His Grandchildren and to Children Everywhere," originally published 1976, https://members.purposefulplanninginstitute.com/wp-content/uploads/2022/04/Sam-Levenson-Ethical-Will.pdf.

Chapter 5: Launching Children
1. Bruce Feiler, "Feel Like You're Lost or Your Life Has Gotten Off Track? How to Begin Again," Ideas.Ted.Com, January 25, 2022, https://ideas.ted.com/mastering-life-transitions-lifequakes-when-youre-lost-or-off-track/.
2. Rabbi Naomi Levy, "A Blessing for a Parent to Say to a Child," in *Talking to God: Personal Prayers for Times of Joy, Sadness, Struggle, and Celebration* (Doubleday, 2002), 97. Adapted by Rabbi Zoë Klein.
3. Adapted from Debbie Friedman, "T'filat Haderech," track 12 on *You Shall Be a Blessing*, Sounds Write, 1997.
4. Rabbi Jonathan Aaron, "2022 Graduation Blessing," Temple Emanuel of Beverly Hills, Beverly Hills, CA.
5. Stuart Kestenbaum, "Joy," in *How to Start Over* (Deerbrook Editions). © 2019 Stuart Kestenbaum. Used by permission of the author.

Chapter 6: Relaunching Ourselves
1. John O'Donohue, "For a New Beginning," in *To Bless the Space Between Us: A Book of Blessings* (Doubleday, 2008), 14.
2. Adapted from Debbie Friedman, "T'filat Haderech," track 12 on *You Shall Be a Blessing*, Sounds Write, 1997.
3. Nora Ephron, "I Feel Bad About My Neck," *New York Times*, August 20, 2006, https://www.nytimes.com/2006/08/20/books/chapters/0820-1st-schi.html.

Chapter 7: Celebrating Friendship
1. John O'Donohue, *Annam Cara: A Book of Celtic Wisdom* (Harper Perennial, 2022), 22.
2. Robert Frost, "Nothing Gold Can Stay," in *The Poetry of Robert Frost*, ed. Edward Connery Lathem (Holt, Rinehart, and Winston, 1969), 222.
3. Rabbi Naamah Kelman, "On Mourning a Friend," in *Getting Good at Getting Older*, by Richard Siegel and Rabbi Laura Geller (Behrman House, 2019), 163–65. © Behrman House, Inc., included with permission, www.Behrmanhouse.com.bless.
4. Rhaina Cohen, *The Other Significant Others: Reimagining Life with Friendship at the Center* (St. Martin's Press, 2024), 23.
5. Sister Joan Chittister, *The Gift of Years: Growing Older Gracefully* (Blue Bridge, 2008), 79.

Chapter 8: Renewing Our Partnership Vows
1. Rainer Maria Rilke, *The Poet's Guide to Life: The Wisdom of Rilke*, trans. Ulrich Baer (Modern Library, 2005), 36.
2. Adapted from "Anniversary: Blessing the Couple," in *L'chol Z'man V'Eit, For Sacred Moments: The CCAR Life-Cycle Guide*, ed. Rabbi Donald Goor (CCAR Press, 2015), Marriage-34.
3. Leah Furnas, "The Longlyweds Know," first published in *To Love One Another: Poems Celebrating Marriage*, by Ginny Lowe Conners (Grayson Books, 2002), 61. Use by permission of Grayson Books.
4. Richard Siegel and Rabbi Laura Geller, *Getting Good at Getting Older* (Behrman House, 2019), 102.

Chapter 9: Becoming a Grandparent/Grandfriend
1. Jerry Witkovsky and Deanna Shoss, *Where Two Worlds Meet: A Guide to Connecting with Your Teenage Grandchildren* (WriteLife Publishing, 2022), 9–10.

2. This ritual can be found at https://jewishgrandparentsnetwork.org/wp-content/uploads/2024/06/Celebrating-Grandparenthood-Water-Pouring-Ceremony-Mayyim-Hayyim-and-JGN.pdf.
3. This ceremony was adapted by Rabbi Amalia Mark for Mayyim Hayyim Living Waters Community Mikveh and Paula Brody & Family Education Center and the Jewish Grandparents Network.
4. Adapted from Leila Gal Berner, "Our Silent Seasons," in *Lifecycles: Jewish Women on Life Passages and Personal Milestones*, vol. 1, ed. Debra Orenstein (Jewish Lights, 1994), 135.
5. Adapted from "Healing Service," Temple Israel of Boston, 2000.
6. Adapted from Rachel Stock Spilker, "70th Birthday Celebration," an immersion ceremony.
7. Marcia Falk, "Blessing of the Children," *The Book of Blessings: New Jewish Prayers for Daily Life, the Sabbath, and the New Moon Festival* (CCAR Press, 2017), 124.
8. Adapted from "Blessing for a Grandchild," in *The New Jewish Baby Book: Names, Ceremonies, and Customs; A Guide for Today's Families*, by Anita Diamant (Jewish Lights/Turner Publishing LLC, 2005), 152. Used by permission.
9. Adapted from "Blessing a Bar/Bat Mitzvah—Family Readings," in *L'chol Z'man V'Eit, For Sacred Moments: The CCAR Life-Cycle Guide*, ed. Rabbi Donald Goor (CCAR Press, 2015), Study-10.
10. "Replay: Marc Freedman Shares Five Things He's Learned About the Power That Comes from Connecting Generations," *Five Things I've Learned* (Substack, October, 20, 2022), https://myfivethings.com/class/marc-freedman-the-power-that-comes-from-connecting-generations/.

Chapter 10: Finalizing a Separation or Divorce

1. Adapted from Rabbi Laura Geller, "Mourning a Marriage," ReformJudaism.org, https://reformjudaism.org/mourning-marriage. Used by permission of Union for Reform Judaism and Rabbi Laura Geller.
2. Judaism includes a category called *mamzer*, which is a child born from forbidden sexual relations such as adultery. A *get* ensures that a marriage is dissolved, and hence future relationships resulting in children cannot be considered adulterous. Sadly, the status of *mamzer* has long-lasting consequences, as it is hereditary and includes restrictions on who a *mamzer* can marry.
3. Jeweler Alison Chemla creates these, as described in https://www.nytimes.com/2024/03/28/style/divorce-ring-wedding-emrata.html.

4. One example is "Divorce & Discovery: A Jewish Healing Retreat," organized by Rabbi Deborah Newbrun, https://www.deborahnewbrun.com.
5. Adapted from Rabbi Rachel Barenblat, "A Ritual for Ending a Marriage," Ritualwell, August 17, 2022, https://ritualwell.org/?s=Barenblat%2C+%E2%80%9CA+Ritual+for+Ending+a+Marriage. Used by permission of the author.
6. Both of these blessings are adapted from Rabbi Lisa Green, *Supplement to L'chol Z'man V'Eit, For Sacred Moments: The CCAR Life-Cycle Guide* (CCAR Press, 2021), Marriage-63.

Chapter 11: Moving Forward After the Death of a Partner
1. Rabbi Chaim Stern, "It Is a Fearful Thing," in *On the Doorposts of Your House: Prayers and Ceremonies for the Jewish Home*, ed. Rabbi Chaim Stern (CCAR Press, 1994), 299.
2. For more about the first year of mourning, see *Navigating the Journey: The Essential Guide to the Jewish Life Cycle*, ed. Rabbi Peter S. Knobel (CCAR Press, 2018).
3. Alfred Huffstickler, "The Cure," in *The Walking Wounded* (Backyard Press, 1989). Used by permission of the Estate of Alfred Huffstickler.
4. Rachel Naomi Remen, *My Grandfather's Blessings: Stories of Strength, Refuge, and Belonging* (Riverhead Books, 2000), 38.
5. Mary Oliver, "In Blackwater Woods," from *American Primitive*, copyright © 1983. Reprinted by permission of Little, Brown, an imprint of Hachette Book Group, Inc.

Chapter 12: Beginning a New Relationship
1. Adapted from Rabbi Richard Address and Andrew L. Rosenkranz, eds., *To Honor and Respect: A Program and Resource Guide for Congregations on Sacred Aging* (URJ Press, 2005).

Chapter 13: Needing Something to Lean On
1. Nessa Rapoport, "Regarding My Body," in *Getting Good at Getting Older*, by Richard Siegel and Rabbi Laura Geller (Behrman House, 2019), 166.
2. Paul Irving, "My Wife Had a Hearing Loss. So Why Wouldn't She Get a Hearing Aid?," *Wall Street Journal*, April 22, 2019, https://www.wsj.com/articles/my-wife-had-hearing-loss-so-why-wouldnt-she-get-a-hearing-aid-01555948110. Reprinted with permission of the Wall Street Journal (2019), Dow Jones Company, Inc. All rights reserved worldwide. License number: 5906680024469.
3. Adapted from by Ilana Schatz, "Ritual for Transitioning to Wheelchair,"

Ritualwell, https://ritualwell.org/ritual/ritual-for-transitioning-to-wheel-chair/.
4. The prayers in the ritual are adapted from Tamara Arnow, "When the Body Begins to Fail: Reaching Out in Prayer," Ritualwell, https://ritualwell.org/ritual/when-body-begins-fail-reaching-out-prayer/.
5. Adapted from Paul Irving, "My Wife Had Hearing Loss."
6. Nancy Mairs, "Challenge: An Exploration," in *Carnal Acts* (Beacon Press, 1996), 104–5.

Chapter 14: Coming Out with Memory Loss

1. "2024 Alzheimer's Disease Facts and Figures: Special Report Mapping a Better Future for Dementia Care Navigation," Alzheimer's Association, 2024, https://www.alz.org/media/Documents/alzheimers-facts-and-figures.pdf.
2. "2024 Alzheimer's Disease Facts and Figures."
3. Adapted from Ariel Neshama Lee, "Prayer for People with Dementia and Their Caregivers," Ritualwell, January 5, 2017, https://ritualwell.org/ritual/prayer-people-dementia-and-their-caregivers/.
4. Rabbi Sheldon Marder, "Upon Receiving a Diagnosis of Dementia," in *Mishkan R'fuah: Where Healing Resides*, ed. Rabbi Eric Weiss (CCAR Press, 2013), 80.
5. Rabbi Eric Weiss, "Facing Dementia," in Weiss, *Mishkan R'fuah*, 81.
6. Rabbi Laura Geller, previously unpublished.
7. Sallie Tisdale, "Out of Time: The Un-becoming of Self," *Harper's Magazine*, March 2018, https://harpers.org/archive/2018/03/out-of-time/.
8. For a more detailed discussion of these issues, see Rabbi Elliot Dorff and Rabbi Laura Geller, "When Alzheimer's Turns a Spouse into a Stranger: Jewish Perspectives of Loving and Letting Go," in *The Sacred Encounter: Jewish Perspectives on Sexuality*, ed. Rabbi Lisa J. Grushcow (CCAR Press, 2014), 549–62.
9. "Ambiguous Loss and Grief in Dementia," Alzheimer's Society of Canada, 2019, https://alzheimer.ca/sites/default/files/documents/ambiguous-loss-and-grief_for-individuals-and-families.pdf.
10. This story was adapted from a chapter originally written by Rabbi Debra R. Hachen for *Sacred Struggle: Jewish Responses to Trauma* (CCAR Press, 2025).
11. Myrna Marofsky, "Let's Change the Conversation Around Dementia," *Next Avenue*, June 20, 2023, https://www.nextavenue.org/lets-change-the-conversation-around-dementia/.

Chapter 15: Becoming a Caregiver or Caregetter

1. Rosalynn Carter, Rosalynn Carter Institute for Caregivers, https://rosalyn-ncarter.org/4kinds/.
2. This ritual is adapted from Matia Rania Angelou and Joyce Friedman, "Healing for Those Supporting Loved Ones with Mental Illness: An Immersion Ceremony," Mayyim Hayyim Living Waters, https://www.mayyimhayyim.org/wp-content/uploads/2020/09/Healing-for-those-Supporting-Loved-Ones-with-Mental-Illness.pdf.
3. This prayer is adapted from a teaching by Rabbi Nancy Flam, untitled lecture, for "Being with What Is: A Silent Jewish Mindfulness Retreat," Institute for Jewish Spirituality, August 15, 2024.
4. For options, please see Rabbi Eric Weiss, ed., *Mishkan R'fuah: Where Healing Resides* (CCAR Press, 2013), 2–9.
5. Adapted from a teaching by Rabbi Nancy Flam, "Being with What Is."
6. Unpublished poem by Rabbi Debra R. Hachen, used with permission.
7. Translated by Rabbi Eric Weiss, "Shehecheyanu," in *Mishkan R'fuah: Where Healing Resides*, ed. Rabbi Eric Weiss (CCAR Press, 2013), 60.
8. Rabbi Rachel Cowan and Dr. Linda Thal, *Wise Aging: Living with Joy, Resilience, and Spirit* (Behrman House, 2015), 135–36. © Behrman House, Inc., included with permission, www.behrmanhouse.com.

Chapter 16: Starting or Ending Medical Treatment

1. Debbie Friedman, "Mourning into Dancing," track 6 on *One People*, JMG/Jewish Music, 2006.
2. Susan Sontag, *Illness as Metaphor* (Vintage Books, 1979), 3.
3. Adapted from Sarah Bunin Benor and Rabbi Shawn Fields-Meyer, "Pre-chemo Upsherin Ceremony," Ritualwell, https://ritualwell.org/ritual/pre-chemo-upsherin-ceremony/.
4. *Asher Yatzar* translation from *Mishkan T'filah: A Reform Siddur* (CCAR Press, 2007), 194.
5. Adapted from Bluma Sussman, "Burning the Cancer Shirts This Passover," Ritualwell, https://ritualwell.org/ritual/burning-the-cancer-shirts-this-passover/.
6. "A Prayer for One Approaching Surgery or Crisis," in *Mishkan R'fuah: Where Healing Resides,* ed. Rabbi Eric Weiss (CCAR Press, 2013), 30, originally published in *Gates of Healing: A Message of Comfort and Hope* (CCAR Press, 1988), 15.

7. This translation is found in the *New Emanuel Minyan Prayer Book*, adapted from Rabbi Avrohom Davis, *The Complete Metsudah Siddur: A New Linear Prayer Book with English Translation* (Metsudah, 1990).

Chapter 17: Saying Goodbye to a Parent's Home

1. Diane Cole, "In Many Houses," in *Kol Haneshamah: Shabbat Vehagim*, 789. Copyright © 1994, The Reconstructionist Press. Used with permission.
2. Adapted from Rabbi Jack Riemer, "A Home Dismantled with Devotion," ReformJudaism.org, https://reformjudaism.org/home-dismantled-devotion. Used by permission of Rabbi Jack Riemer, Sharon Davidson, and Union of Reform Judaism.
3. Marie Ponsot, "As Is," in *Collected Poems*, compilation copyright © 2016 by Marie Ponsot, 91. Used by permission of Alfred A. Knopf, an imprint of the Knopf Doubleday Publishing Group, a division of Penguin Random House LLC. All rights reserved.
4. Rabbi Jonathan Sacks, *The Chief Rabbi's Haggadah: Hebrew and English Text with New Essays and Commentary* (Harper Collins, 2003), 29.

Chapter 18: Decluttering or Downsizing Your Home

1. Alan Morinis, *Everyday Holiness: The Jewish Spiritual Path of Mussar* (Trumpeter, 2007), 115.
2. Rabbi Karyn D. Kedar, *Amen: Seeking Presence with Prayer, Poetry, and Mindfulness* (CCAR Press, 2020), 53.

Chapter 19: Leaving Your Home

1. Translation from *The JPS Tanakh: Gender-Sensitive Edition* (Jewish Publication Society, 2023), found on Sefaria (sefaria.org).
2. Adapted from Rebecca Van Wagner, "Ritual for Moving Out of a Home," Ritualwell, https://ritualwell.org/ritual/ritual-for-moving-out-of-a-home/.
3. Translation by the authors.
4. Adapted from Debbie Friedman, "T'filat Haderech," track 12 on *You Shall Be a Blessing*, Sounds Write, 1997.
5. Rabbi Michael Howald, "When a Student Completes a Book of Talmud," adapted. Used by permission of the author.

Chapter 20: Moving into a New Community and a New Home

1. Mary Oliver, "The Place I Want to Get Back To." Reprinted by the permission of The Charlotte Sheedy Literary Agency as agent for the author. Copyright © 2006 by Mary Oliver with permission of Bill Reichblum.

2. Adapted from "Consecration of a House," in *On the Doorposts of Your House: Prayers and Ceremonies for the Jewish Home*, ed. Rabbi Chaim Stern (CCAR Press, 1994), 138–40.
3. Rabbi Rachel Barenblat, "A Prayer for Entering Assisted Living," in "Transitions to Supported Living," Jewish Doorways, https://jewishdoorways.org/stage_events/transition-to-assisted-living-or-nursing-home/. Used by permission of the author.
4. Unknown author, "*Birkat HaBayit*," trans. Aharon N. Varady, The Open Siddur Project, November 18, 2015 (license: CC-BY-SA 4.0, https://creativecommons.org/licenses/by-sa/4.0/), found on https://opensiddur.org/prayers/life-cycle/living/home/birkat-habayit-blessing-for-the-home/.

A Concluding Thought
1. Adapted, with permission, from Rabbi Marc Margolius.

About the Authors

Rabbi Laura Geller, rabbi emerita of Temple Emanuel of Beverly Hills, was the third woman in the Reform Movement to become a rabbi. Named one of *Newsweek*'s 50 Most Influential Rabbis in America and by PBS's *Next Avenue* as a 2017 Influencer in Aging, she was a cofounder of Chai VillageLA and is the chair of the Synagogue Village Network. She served on the Corporation of Brown University, from where she graduated in 1971, and on the board of the Jewish Women's Archive. Currently she serves on the boards of CoGenerate (CoGenerate.org; formerly Encore.org), and the Active Aging Resource Network (ActiveAgingNetwork.org; formerly B3/The Jewish Boomer Platform). She was featured in the PBS documentary *Jewish Americans*, is the author of numerous articles in books and journals, and was on the editorial board of *The Torah: A Women's Commentary*. Her book *Getting Good at Getting Older*, coauthored with her husband Richard Siegel, z"l, was named a National Jewish Book Award finalist in the category of Contemporary Jewish Life and Practice. She is the mother of Joshua and Elana Goldstein, the stepmother of Andy and Ruth Siegel, the grateful mother-in-law of Janelle Goldstein, Zach Rausnitz, and Will Swanson, and the very proud *savta* of Avery, Levi, Phoebe, Alice, and Nell. Please visit her website at www.rabbilaurageller.com.

Rabbi Beth Lieberman is passionate about growth and innovation in Jewish life. She has served both the Reform and Conservative Movements, organizing and building multigenerational faith communities, and her work in the literary world in the areas of Jewish scholarship, culture, and practice has received national acclaim. She serves as adjunct faculty at the Hebrew Union College–Jewish Institute of Religion, School of Rabbinical Studies, in Los Angeles, mentoring the next generation of communal leaders. Her writings have appeared in numerous publications, and she has written and taught widely about her role as literary editor and a revising translator of the *JPS Hebrew-English Tanakh: Revised Edition* (Jewish Publication Society and Sefaria.org, 2023). She lives with her family in California, dividing her time between Los Angeles and New York. Please visit her website at www.rabbibethlieberman.com.

www.ingramcontent.com/pod-product-compliance
Lightning Source LLC
Chambersburg PA
CBHW061303110426
42742CB00012BA/2038